HENRY MILLER

Literature and Life: American Writers

Selected list of titles:

SAUL BELLOW	*Brigitte Scheer-Schäzler*
TRUMAN CAPOTE	*Helen S. Garson*
RACHEL CARSON	*Carol B. Gartner*
THEODORE DREISER	*James Lundquist*
WILLIAM FAULKNER	*Alan Warren Friedman*
F. SCOTT FITZGERALD	*Rose Adrienne Gallo*
ROBERT FROST	*Elaine Barry*
LILLIAN HELLMAN	*Doris V. Falk*
ERNEST HEMINGWAY	*Samuel Shaw*
JOHN IRVING	*Gabriel Miller*
THE NOVELS OF HENRY JAMES	*Edward Wagenknecht*
THE TALES OF HENRY JAMES	*Edward Wagenknecht*
KEN KESEY	*Barry H. Leeds*
MARY MCCARTHY	*Willene Schaefer Hardy*
JAMES A. MICHENER	*George J. Becker*
ANAÏS NIN	*Bettina L. Knapp*
JOHN O'HARA	*Robert Emmet Long*
THE PLAYS OF EUGENE O'NEILL	*Virginia Floyd*
EDGAR ALLAN POE	*Bettina L. Knapp*
J.D. SALINGER	*James Lundquist*
JOHN STEINBECK	*Paul McCarthy*
LIONEL TRILLING	*Edward Joseph Shoben, Jr.*
MARK TWAIN	*Robert Keith Miller*
NATHANAEL WEST	*Robert Emmet Long*
THORNTON WILDER	*David Castronovo*
EDMUND WILSON	*David Castronovo*
RICHARD WRIGHT	*David Bakish*

Complete list of titles in the series available from publisher on request. Some titles are also in paperback.

HENRY MILLER

J.D. Brown

UNGAR • NEW YORK

1986

The Ungar Publishing Company
370 Lexington Avenue
New York, N.Y. 10017

Copyright © 1986 by The Ungar Publishing Company

Printed in the United States of America

Library of Congress Cataloging-in-Publication Data

Brown, J. D. (James Dale), 1948-
  Henry Miller.

  (Literature and life series)
  Bibliography: p.
  Includes index.
  1. Miller, Henry, 1891–   —Criticism and
interpretation. I. Title. II. Series.
PS3525.I5454Z659   1986   818'.5209   86–6961
ISBN 0-8044-2077-7

To the inseparable Sherpa,
and Margaret,
who makes dreams possible

Contents

Chronology

composes outline of what will become *The Rosy Crucifixion* trilogy and begins second novel (*Moloch* —never published).

1928   Tours Europe and Paris with June. Returns to New York.

1929   Begins third, more overtly autobiographical novel (*Crazy Cock*—never published).

1930   Begins expatriation alone in Paris. Meets Alfred Perlès.

1931   Begins *Tropic of Cancer*. Meets Anaïs Nin. Publishes in *New Review*, Paris.

1932   Works as proofreader on Paris edition of *Chicago Tribune*. Begins a book on D. H. Lawrence.

1933   Lives with Alfred Perlès in Clichy.

1934   Publishes *Tropic of Cancer* in Paris, September 1. Moves to 18, Villa Seurat. Divorces June, September 20.

1935   Returns to New York City. Works as lay analyst with Anaïs Nin, Otto Rank. Back in Paris, broke, he publishes two epistolary works, *What Are You Going to Do about Alf?* and *Aller Retour New York*. Begins "Hamlet" correspondence with Michael Fraenkel.

1936   Publishes *Black Spring* in Paris.

1937   Meets Lawrence Durrell. Edits "Villa Seurat Library" (books by Durrell, Nin, Miller).

1938   Publishes *Max and the White Phagocytes* in Paris.

1939   Publishes *Tropic of Capricorn* in Paris. Leaves Paris, May 31. Stays with Durrell in Greece. *The Cosmological Eye* (a version of *Max and the White Phagocytes*) published in America by New Directions.

1940   Arrives in New York City, January 12. Writes *Quiet Days in Clichy, The World of Sex*, and *The Colossus of Maroussi*, all initially rejected by American publishers.

1

New York:
Early Sorrows

Henry Miller is the late-bloomer of modern literature. He began his career as a writer later than his contemporaries, and even then he had to wait a generation or more to be widely read. In 1934 he was a forty-three-year-old expatriate American writer in Paris who had failed to make his mark in the literary world, and for good reason: his previous writing showed no originality, power, or promise. He subsisted on the handouts of strangers and the leftovers from a few friends. The same year, however, with the appearance of his first book, *Tropic of Cancer*, he suddenly secured a vast international following. Yet his sudden celebrity did not enrich him nor win him many readers. *Tropic of Cancer* was immediately banned as pornographic in every country except France. In the popular mind, the name of the author was synonymous with obscenity in literature. The embargo on *Tropic of Cancer* would last almost thirty years, and by the time it was published in America, becoming the year's best seller, Miller was seventy years old.

The passages in *Tropic of Cancer* that were sufficient to shock readers and rally censors of past generations now seem quite tame. The reason is that the court decisions lifting the ban on Miller's work have shaped what is acceptable in our literature today. *Tropic of Cancer* completed the moral redefinition initiated by two

other, once notorious classics, James Joyce's *Ulysses* and
D. H. Lawrence's *Lady Chatterley's Lover*; but, to a
greater extent than in these previous landmark cases,
Miller's pioneering treatment of human experience
would obscure an appreciation of his more lasting, innovative literary achievements.

From the first, a surprising number of prominent
writers discerned Miller's importance as a writer. The
young British novelist Lawrence Durrell immediately
embraced *Tropic of Cancer* as "the copy-book for my
generation." The elder statesman of Anglo-American
poetry, T. S. Eliot, hailed it as a "remarkable book . . . a
rather magnificent piece of work" that was "a great deal
better in depth of insight and of course in the actual writing than *Lady Chatterley's Lover*." Ezra Pound, the supreme critic of modernism, assured Miller that he had
made a more important contribution to literature than
had Virginia Woolf. *Tropic of Cancer*, Pound said, "out-
Ulyssed Joyce." Edwin Muir, a more sober critic, believed that Miller's narrative pierced "deeper into the
disease of our existence than any other" and was "a work
of genius, terrifying and comic." Even George Orwell,
who objected to Miller's lack of political commitment,
regarded him as "the only imaginative prose-writer of
the slightest value who has appeared among the English-
speaking races for some years past." Orwell went so far
as to predict that "in the remaining years of free speech
any novel worth reading will follow more or less along
the lines that Miller has followed."[1]

Such high praise, no doubt exaggerated by the censorship issues of the time, suggested that there was more
to Miller's work than the attractions of the risqué. Here
might be a serious literary artist, unread, shackled by a
moribund morality. Turning the debate to his advan-
tage, Miller posed as a desperado, a down-and-out icon-
oclast, the Great American Anarchist. He became the
center of a vigorous circle opposed to the "tired" literary

establishment. For decades, discussions of Miller were polarized. Dispassionate criticism was scant: he was either adored or reviled.

In the fifty years since the publication of *Tropic of Cancer*, the issues of censorship and artistic freedom have cooled; Henry Miller is now recognized as a major American writer. Assessing the magnitude and nature of his literary achievement, however, remains difficult, if no longer impossible. It has long been held that his works do not fit into the leading categories of twentieth-century literature; but the key to categorization is in Miller's remark to Edmund Wilson about *Tropic of Cancer*: "I am the hero and the book is me."[2] Miller is not writing novels, letters, or essays, primarily; he is writing new versions of autobiography. To measure his achievement, the reader must consider the distinguished American tradition in autobiography, in which Miller is a major figure.

Unlike Benjamin Franklin or Henry Adams, Miller wrote his autobiography in several modes simultaneously. In the narrative mode, he wrote about his life in New York in the twenties, Paris in the thirties, Greece at the beginning of the World War, and California in the fifties. In the discursive mode, he added personal essays, literary criticism, and accounts of travel where the subject was almost invariably himself. In the epistolary mode, in which he was particularly prolific, Miller expanded his correspondence (sometimes even a single letter) into books which again were centrally concerned with the actual experience of the author. The literary achievement in each of these modes is uneven, but the overall effect is monumental. No writer since Whitman has expressed as fully as Miller the essential experiences of the individual artist in autobiographical form.

In creating his twentieth-century autobiography, Miller drew upon the narrative strategies of modern fiction. He introduced surrealism, dadaism, and dark humor to the autobiographical form, with savage results. "One has to take the English language back to Marlowe and Shakespeare," notes Norman Mailer, "before encountering a wealth of imagery equal in intensity." In addition to innovative techniques, Miller fashioned a fresh, authentic style, perhaps the most distinctive personal voice in the vernacular tradition since Mark Twain's. "Few writers in the history of literature speak with so powerful a presence," Norman Mailer observes. "Miller at his best wrote a prose grander than Faulkner's, and wilder. Men with literary styles as full as Hawthorne's appear by comparison stripped of their rich language."[3] Miller's mastery of the colloquial voice and surrealistic style was not always firm; his prose could suddenly sink to self-indulgent bombast. When Miller was bad, he was very bad; but when he controlled his strategies—as he first did in *Tropic of Cancer*—the extremes of language, emotion, and idea fused perfectly. He recast autobiographical form for the twentieth century. His prose became very good indeed.

Miller loved extremes, in art and in life; furthermore, in him the autobiographical impulse was so complete that the usual distinctions between art and life were all but obliterated. As the critic William Gordon remarks, "For the autobiographical writer, his own life, his own views, his triumphs and defeats are not only the stuff of his art, they are the stuff of life."[4] This identification of art and life can produce, in the view of Ihab Hassan, "autobiography of a special kind" in which the artist denies art and all literary forms. If life itself proves anarchistic, then so must the forms of its expression. Miller, "the first author of anti-literature," approaches the "act of pure self-expression" in which literary form disappears.[5] Indeed, Miller's intent is often antiliterary. His work sometimes lacks traditional structure and *mesure*. Yet it is obvious that his best narration is organized—it is, in fact, highly literary.

When in 1957, despite the continuing worldwide ban on his best work, Miller was elected to the National Institute of Arts and Letters, Louise Bogan praised both content and method, both the "boldness of approach and intense curiosity" and the "originality and richness of technique."[6] In the first forty years of Miller's life, however, there was little to suggest that he would possess any of these qualities, nor that he would one day become America's most important modern autobiographical writer.

Henry Miller was born on December 26, 1891, near York Avenue in Manhattan. The next year his family moved and Henry became, as he later said, "just a Brooklyn boy." The son of second-generation immigrants, Henry could speak only German until he began school. His father, Heinrich, a tailor, was an easygoing raconteur; his mother, Louise, was a stern perfectionist who alternately spoiled and punished her son. After high school, Henry attended City College for two months, dropped out, and drifted from one job to the next without enthusiasm. Aimlessness became the pattern of his youth. He read voraciously, and by age twenty knew he wanted to write stories, but a few attempts at authorship completely discouraged him. Still, there was kindled an autobiographical impulse: "Some day I will write an enormous, ultimate book in which everything will be recorded . . . all, all my life," Miller promised himself.[7]

A decisive event in Miller's wanderings came during a disastrous trip to California. There he met Emma Goldman briefly, and this set him to reading Nietzsche, Hamsun, and other Europeans. Miller's anarchism was not political, but he admired Goldman's approach to life; her emphasis on personal freedom reaffirmed what Miller had admired in Jack London and Walt Whitman.

In 1917 Miller married an older woman, Beatrice Sylvas Wickens. It was not a happy union. They had a daughter two years later. Miller reached print with a half dozen brief "reader's reviews" in *The Black Cat*, a small story magazine published in Salem, Massachusetts, but otherwise he did not further his literary ambitions.

Finally in 1920 Miller talked his way into a relatively high-paying, long-term position as an employment manager for Western Union Telegraph Company. Immediately he saw the extent of suffering endured by those at the bottom of industrial America, and he repudiated the institutions he thought created misery. He decided to write a novel of social protest ridiculing the success myth popularized by Horatio Alger novels; he would present portraits of twelve messengers who were destroyed by the system. Modeled after Theodore Dreiser's didactic novel, *Twelve Men*, Miller's book, *Clipped Wings*, was abominable: the style was arch, the approach doctrinaire, the characters no more substantial than cardboard. He typed out the entire manuscript over a three-week vacation from Western Union. March 20, 1922, was Miller's "first day of being a writer," as he proclaimed in a letter to Emil Schnellock, and it "has nearly broken my back." Miller wrote five thousand words in his first eight hours—and he rightly expressed "grave doubts" about the result.[8]

A year later Miller divorced his first wife, lost custody of his daughter, and met June Edith Smith Mansfield, the woman who would become his second wife. June would also become the "dark woman" of his autobiographical romances, the irresistible femme fatale who created herself anew moment by moment. After marrying June, and at her urging, Miller abruptly quit his job to devote himself solely to writing; but he could produce nothing of consequence. In imitation of Walt Whitman, he composed several dozen prose-poems. Printed as broadsides, these were dubbed mezzotints, and June sold them to her gentlemen admirers. The Millers opened a speakeasy in Greenwich Village, but it, too, produced no income. That same year, 1925, Miller hitchhiked to Florida with two friends to strike it rich in the real-estate boom. He returned home in December, broke. On his thirty-fifth birthday, he declared himself a complete failure as a writer and a man, but he was to sink deeper.[9] By April 1927 he was working as a grave-digger for the Queens County Park Commission; his wife was touring Paris with a lesbian avant-garde poet (on money supplied by one of her male admirers); and Miller had written only a twenty-six-page outline of an epic about his four years with June (a work that he would not finish for forty years).

Somehow Miller pushed himself on as a writer. He reworked his Western Union novel, retitled *Moloch*, and made himself the manager—hero of the messenger service. He added more earthiness to the narrative, but the writing remained stiff, derivative, and unpublish-able. One of June's moneyed admirers liked the manu-script (or liked June, who passed it off as her own work) enough to act as patron. He sent the Millers to Europe in 1928, where they stayed nearly a year, ostensibly to polish their novel. Curiously, Miller hated Paris. He could not write. Paris in 1928 was merely another point-less stop.

In 1929, however, Miller started a third novel, *Crazy Cock*, which was closer to the autobiographical form and a more promising narrative. At June's insis-tence, Miller returned alone to Paris to write, again with an admirer's money. He arrived on March 4, 1930. Vir-tually penniless, his situation quickly worsened. As an aspiring middle-aged expatriate writer, he was twenty years too late to participate in the fabulous Hemingway-Fitzgerald exile. Yet his exile lasted the entire decade.

Paris in the Depression years was not the magical center of modern art and literature, but it transformed Henry Miller into a writer of the first rank. There he was able to write that "enormous, ultimate book" he had promised to himself as a young man. Once *Tropic of Cancer* took shape, Miller began his "long elaboration of autobiography."[10] He did not cease writing until his death fifty years later.

2

▼▼

Paris:
Birth of a Writer

It was in exile that Henry Miller found himself as a writer. Paris at its most unsavory strengthened him; poverty, desperation, and loneliness lent distinct shapes to his fierce, creative energies. Miller began to write almost exclusively about his immediate life. He found the process of living day to day in Paris identical to the process of writing. Both were acts of desperation; both required that he master the basic elements of survival. Paris was for Miller the place where the most extreme opposites coalesced, where the most sordid experiences were charged with transcendent value. Finding life and art indistinguishable, Miller naturally turned from writing novels to creating new forms of autobiography. He celebrated Paris as no other writer of the decade would.

In fact, however, Miller had little to celebrate. When, at age thirty-eight, he arrived in Paris on March 4, 1930, he was twenty years too late. His famous contemporaries—Hemingway, Fitzgerald, Dos Passos, and a host of other American expatriates—had come and gone. Paris was not the same. Miller himself was unknown and unaccomplished. His only income was the ten dollars he had borrowed from Emil Schnellock in New York.

Miller had no choice but to walk the streets. It was there that *Tropic of Cancer* took shape. Miller wrote accounts of his first impressions to Emil. The letters were

long and deliberately literary. As George Wickes notes,
Miller's spontaneous letters to Emil served as his writer's
workshop. Many sections of these letters would appear
later in *Tropic of Cancer* with but slight revisions. Miller's adventures with the local characters and prostitutes
of Montparnasse, his fresh response to the events of the
day, his surrealistic rendering of Parisian street life were
all worked out in letters before being redrawn in narrative form.[1]

Miller's letters of 1930 document the exuberance of
an impoverished expatriate. *Tropic of Cancer* was to
have a wealth of literal as well as literary sources. While
Miller's actual circumstances were dire—he had no
close friends, no job, almost no money, and no fixed
residence—he was able to convert the essence of his
hand-to-mouth existence into a voracious celebration of
basic existence. Living in seedy hotels, panhandling in
the streets, haunting the cafés—everything fueled Miller's joyous outbursts. On the first page of *Tropic of Cancer* he would compress his new vision into a few words:
"I have no money, no resources, no hopes. I am the hap-
piest man alive."[2]

June had promised to wire him money, but it seldom came. Miller soon pawned the suits tailored at his
father's shop. He moved to less expensive hotels. He
begged for handouts from American tourists. An indefat-
igable walker, Miller explored the seamier avenues of
Paris. Desperate for money, he started to write a guide-
book, but he could now only write in the first person.
His concern was himself, his survival. Anything but an
autobiographical approach would falsify his experience.

After just a month abroad, Miller was down to his
last franc, and he probably would have returned to
America had he not met Alfred Perlès, an Austrian
writer with an inglorious past. In an engaging but
unreliable reminiscence composed with Miller's assistance, Perlès recounts their first meeting in Paris at a

sidewalk café. Absolutely penniless, Miller piles saucer upon saucer at his table as he deliberates on how best to evade paying his mounting tab. He engages Perlès in a long conversation, and Perlès ends up paying Miller's bill. "Like Henry, I had been destitute and hungry; like him, I had managed to survive," Perlès explains. "The situations he had to face I had had to face as well: we had developed the same desperado philosophy."[3] Perlès would be Miller's closest friend in Paris, a kindred soul who always came to the rescue.

Dozens of Miller's actual experiences were patched into the "fictional" narrative of *Tropic of Cancer*. His constant need for money and sustenance found expression in the urgent rhythms of his prose. Surrealism and dadaism came naturally, too. Perlès introduced Miller to the work of Blaise Cendrars, André Breton, and Philippe Soupault, but Miller was already experimenting with his own version of surrealism. As a literary technique, it comported with Miller's own vision of his life in Paris; it was also for Miller a means of liberation from the literary *isms* of the age. His goal was to write as no other writer had ever done and to write about what no one else had ever dared.

By the end of summer, however, Miller had sunk even deeper into despair, experiencing a sense of hopelessness more complete than any he had previously imagined. He hung on only because June promised to arrive. She came to Paris in October, replete with dreams of becoming a Parisian cinema star. Those dreams collapsed in a month and June left in November, but Henry stayed. "Slowly he began to realize that Paris was good for him," Jay Martin, Miller's biographer, suggests, "because it was a slaughter-house of dreams, a perfect zero. The only law in Paris was—reality."[4] It was the harsh reality Miller needed to give his literary work its savage force. Rather than reject the miserable life he led, Miller embraced it.

Nevertheless, facing a dreadful winter, alone and penniless, Miller tried to raise enough money to leave Paris. When he failed, he finally accepted his fate. Then, for once, Miller was lucky. He was introduced to Richard Osborn, a Yale Law School graduate who worked at a bank by day and led a riotous life by night among the idle rich of Bohemia. Osborn kept a large apartment at 2, rue Auguste-Bartholdi near the Eiffel Tower, and there Miller spent the winter in comfort, entirely at Osborn's expense.

Richard Osborn, who appears as Fillmore in *Tropic of Cancer*, has written his own account of life with Miller, and it agrees substantially with Miller's narrative. Miller worked at the typewriter nearly every day and soon composed his first successful story, "Mademoiselle Claude," a portrait of his relationship with Germaine Daugeard, a prostitute. Although it lacked the fierce vision and bite of later works, this first-person story contains the hard-boiled sentimentality and low-life subject matter characteristic of Henry Miller's art. Samuel Putnam, an American expatriate writer, editor, and translator, accepted "Mademoiselle Claude" for the Fall 1931 issue of his *New Review*.[5]

In the spring of 1931, Miller again shared an apartment with Alfred Perlès. Always resourceful, he now devised an ingenious meal schedule whereby he secured a complimentary dinner each day, rotating among seven friends. This sustained him until he landed a position as a twelve-dollar-a-week proofreader on the European edition of the *Chicago Tribune*, where Perlès worked, a job which would become the basis for several of the best dadaistic episodes of *Tropic of Cancer*.

During his brief stint with the *Tribune*, Miller made several important friends. One was Walter Lowenfels, an American poet. Lowenfels was involved in a philosophical discussion of death with another writer, Michael Fraenkel. Miller became a third party.

In June 1931 he moved in with Fraenkel at 18, Villa Seurat. Fraenkel's influence was irresistible at first, but Miller finally concluded that the death instinct was not an end in itself, but a means to rebirth. Rejecting Fraenkel's abstract formulation of universal cataclysm, Miller sought personal resurrection in a world of death. Fraenkel appears in *Tropic of Cancer* as Boris, the prophet of death, paralyzed by introspection; by contrast, Miller portrays himself as the prophet of the sensuous life, submerged in the vital stream of experiences. The first episode of *Tropic of Cancer* burlesques Miller's life with Fraenkel, which came to an abrupt end when Fraenkel sublet 18, Villa Seurat in July 1931.

Shortly afterwards, Miller and Perlès joined forces as literary editors. Samuel Putnam entrusted them with the galleys of the *New Review* while in New York on business. Miller immediately sabotaged the issue, tossing out Robert McAlmon's lead story and attaching a manifesto, "The New Instinctivism." In this parody of the literary manifesto, Miller and Perlès proclaimed their opposition to all movements and *isms* and their wholehearted support of complete, "irresponsible" liberation. This revolution was quelled, without recrimination, by Putnam. A version of the event is included in *Tropic of Cancer*; Putnam appears as Marlowe, the drunken scholar.

Miller meanwhile was refining his own image, both as the down-and-out American in Paris and as the hero of his own writing. "Henry began to create a character whom he dubbed himself," Jay Martin observes. "Squarely in the center of his literary work was this figure of a vagabond artist, reckless and irresponsible, childish and thoroughly unscrupulous; pulsating with sensuous vigor, but also zany, always on the edge of insanity; saintly, but ready to become a criminal at the slightest provocation."[6] Miller deliberately cultivated this image of himself as the Romantic artist. If the brutal

necessities of life in Paris produced the anecdotal structure, savage content, and Dionysian hero of Miller's art,
the author was also not above transforming his dismal
condition into a means of self-promotion. On every occasion, Miller presented himself as the expatriate
clochard, the picaresque desperado. Wambly Bald,
whose weekly column, "La Vie Boheme," reported the
gossip of Montparnasse, once allowed Miller to
ghostwrite a self-portrait. The result appeared under
Bald's byline in the 14 October 1931 European edition of
the *Chicago Tribune*, where Miller portrayed himself as
a happy-go-lucky "legitimate child of Montparnasse, the
salt of the quarter," who boldly conned Bald into giving
him a handout.

In September, June wrote that she was miserable
without Henry and would return to Paris. Henry was
more bewildered than bewitched by the news. He had
just been introduced to a young woman who would replace June in his affections, Anaïs Nin. Osborn had provided the contact; Hugh Guiler, Nin's husband, was
Osborn's superior at the bank. Opposites in many ways,
Henry Miller and Anaïs Nin were immediately attracted
to each other. Henry had already visited Anaïs a few
times in Louveciennes, a quiet village west of Paris on
the Seine. When June arrived in October, Miller had
just given Nin a few pages of his manuscript for *Tropic of
Cancer*. Now he wrote not only of June's arrival, but of
his fear that his work would offend Anaïs:

I shall probably bring the remaining pages and some diary
notes and letters along, if that will interest you. I want you to
be interested. I feel very warmly the hospitality, the sympathy
and friendliness you have shown toward me. At the same time
I feel very sensitive—a fear of being misunderstood, or something perhaps less definitive and crude than that but akin. I
don't want to be thought of as having a dirty mind. On the
other hand, I don't wish to palliate the writing, to make a de-

fense, etc. I want it to stand (or fall) on its own merits. I know
that it will reveal a great deal about me.[7]

In this, Miller's first letter to Nin, there is a formality
that would soon disappear. June sensed the threat, but
she soon found the situation complicated when Anaïs
made advances toward her. By Christmas Eve, June was
demanding a divorce, and Nin arranged for Miller to become an English instructor at the Lycée Carnot, a pre-
paratory school in Dijon. Once Henry was out of Paris,
June left for America. Thereafter Anaïs became the most
important figure in Miller's life. In 1932 they exchanged
over nine hundred letters, but their relationship was
more than epistolary.

While the Henry-Anaïs-June triangle is not treated
in *Tropic of Cancer*, Miller's teaching job at Dijon is the
basis of a major episode. The position paid little, the fa-
cilities were spartan, the curriculum uninspired, and
Miller longed for Paris. Dijon was a nightmare, and so
Miller would render it later, in shades dark enough to rival those of Poe. Nin sent several lavish gifts to Henry in
Dijon, but he lasted just two months. In the spring he
moved in with Perlès at 4, avenue Anatole France in
Clichy, where Nin paid Miller's share of the rent.

Finally, in the summer of 1932, the last episode recounted in *Tropic of Cancer* transpired. Osborn had a
nervous breakdown, brought on in part by the preg-
nancy of a young French girl he had taken in. Coming to
his former benefactor's aid, Miller deftly steered Osborn
out of the clutches of an angry mother and the French
authorities. After shipping home the besieged American
expatriate, Miller pocketed the money Osborn had
meant for the young woman.

The real-life bases of Miller's literary masterpiece
were complete. All that remained were some extensive
but manageable revisions and the discovery of a willing

publisher. A publisher quickly appeared—Jack Kahane, an English expatriate who owned the Obelisk Press. Kahane was notorious in Paris. His press specialized in risqué novels, some composed by the publisher himself. Obelisk Press had also released serious, if controversial, works such as Frank Harris's *My Life and Loves*.

Kahane's judgment of *Tropic of Cancer* was enthusiastic. "I had read the most terrible, the most sordid, the most magnificent manuscript that had ever fallen into my hands," he recalled later. "Nothing I had yet received was comparable to it for the splendor of its writing, the fathomless depth of its despair, the savour of its portraiture, the boisterousness of its humour."[8] Even so, it would be two years before Kahane published *Tropic of Cancer*. He repeatedly stalled Miller, fearing the wrath of French censors. Frustrated, Miller initiated a series of new literary projects, only to be interrupted by a third, and as it turned out final, visit from June. Anaïs Nin eventually paid June's return passage to America on December 26, 1932, the day Henry turned forty-one years old.

Miller owed a great debt to Nin, as he often acknowledged. She had constantly encouraged him, supported him financially, and introduced him to a wider spectrum of European culture. On the surface, the two writers are an unlikely pair. As Gunther Stuhlmann points out, Miller "gorged himself with the world around him, the world of dirty streets and dirty people, and spat it out again—transformed, vitalized, reborn in a twentieth-century manner no writer before him had achieved," while Nin "sought to probe for the reality behind the surface, the reality of dream and the endless facets of character." Nin created a world far more "harmonious, beautiful, colorful and richly textured" than the one Miller amalgamated and caricatured. Nevertheless, there were deeper affinities. Both writers rejected the conventional methods of creative expression, ignored dominant new literary movements, and adopted none of the political ideologies that shaped other works of the period.[9] Seeking new literary forms, Nin and Miller created new autobiographical forms.

Hoping to lend respectability and prestige to Henry Miller's name, Kahane insisted that Miller write a study of D. H. Lawrence to precede publication of *Tropic of Cancer*. For most of 1933, Miller was swamped as he prepared his Lawrence book; he failed ever to organize his materials in a coherent manner. Meanwhile, Anaïs Nin was impatient to see *Tropic of Cancer* in print, and she raised six hundred dollars to underwrite its publication. Despite her extraordinary efforts, it did not appear until September 1, 1934, the very day the author moved back into an apartment at 18, Villa Seurat where he had begun what he had called three years earlier "an album of my Paris life."

Tropic of Cancer consists of fifteen episodes in rough chronological order, but the progression of time and development of character are not emphasized. Rather, events and characters are designed to demonstrate that time is fragmentary and disintegrating. All order in the world, and western civilization itself, is collapsing. Only the autonomous self, called Henry Miller in the narrative, remains whole, accepting and encouraging universal destruction. The book alternates first-person narrative and exposition, as autobiographies traditionally do, but Miller has added to the genre all the techniques of fiction, including surrealism. *Tropic of Cancer* is the first major autobiography to incorporate such substantial portions of novelistic technique and poetic organization, confirming the modern view that autobiography is "in effect a novel written in the present, with one's past as its subject."[10]

In Miller's autobiography in the guise of a novel, the theme is death—"the cancer of time is eating us away," the narrator-hero-author declares—but the vision is of personal liberation in a dark time (p. 1). Using a rhetoric of violence, Miller makes Paris his modern Walden, but the epitaph for *Tropic of Cancer* could well be the same that Thoreau used a century earlier: "I do not propose to write an ode to dejection, but to brag as lustily as chanticleer in the morning, standing on his roost, if only to wake my neighbors up." Miller's twentieth-century version of the transcendental artist's task is, it is true, phrased more savagely: "to overthrow existing values, to make of the chaos about him an order which is his own, to sow strife and ferment so that by the emotional release those who are dead may be restored to life" (p. 228). Like Thoreau, Miller has left his place of birth "to front only the essential facts of life," and although the facts may now be sordid and even obscene, Miller will not shy away from the most basic experiences of his age. He shares Thoreau's bold, ultimately transcendental desire: "I wanted to live deep and suck out all the marrow of life," Thoreau explained in *Walden*, "to live so sturdily and Spartan-like as to put to rout all that was not life, to cut a broad swath and shave close, to drive life into a corner, and reduce it to its lowest terms, and, if it proved to be mean, why then to get the whole and genuine meanness of it, and publish its meanness to the world; or if it were sublime, to know it by experience, and be able to give a true account of it."[11]

Tropic of Cancer, then, is a twentieth-century Walden in so far as Miller does suck out the marrow of a marginal life, puts to rout everything that seems lifeless or sterile (which is most of the modern industrial world), cuts a wide anarchistic and romantic swath, and reduces life to both its meanest and its most transcendent terms. Miller portrays each event in harsh, naturalistic detail, then transforms the sordid and grotesque into a "fantasia of associated images which provide a raging or joyous escape from the limiting reality."[12] To bridge dark reality and luminous self-discovery, Miller uses the technique of the surrealists. This literary technique comes to stand for the moral and visionary process by which an individual can transcend a world of death. As a whole, *Tropic of Cancer* is exactly what Anaïs Nin said it was in her preface (written in collaboration with Miller), "a book which, if such a thing were possible, might restore our appetite for the fundamental realities." This revitalization, moral as well as aesthetic, depends on Miller's announced intention to "paint a pre-Socratic being, a creature part goat, part Titan" that will become the imaginative and human model for a "resurrection of the emotions" (p. 220).

Although plot and structure are deliberately suppressed in *Tropic of Cancer*, since they represent a false, outdated order, they exist in submerged form. The structure is not unlike that favored by American Romantics and transcendentalists, particularly Whitman—which is to say organic and natural. Four seasons underlie Miller's episodic and shifting narrative. He begins in the fall, recounting his life and visions while living with Boris (Michael Fraenkel) at the Villa Borghese (Villa Seurat). The narrative is immediate, continuous with the present, but the past and future are also evoked. In the third episode, in Miller's sentimental portrait of the prostitute Germaine, sexuality is treated as an element of revitalization and transcendence. Elsewhere, when sexuality is reduced to mechanical or biological lust, as it is for other characters, then intercourse becomes the occasion for meditations on death-in-life. By the fourth episode, it is spring, Easter day in fact, and Miller, in tune with nature as well as the sensuous instincts, finds himself "incurably optimistic and healthy" (pp. 45–46). He has no sorrows or regrets, no past or future. "The present is enough for me. Day by day. Today!" he declares (p. 46). There is an account of Miller and Carl's (Perlès's) aborted effort to take over Marlowe's (Samuel Putnam's) literary magazine. This is followed by Miller's adventures as a dinner guest being rotated among his more prosperous friends. At the end of the fifth episode, the hero identifies with the river Seine—"I don't know what it is rushes up in me at the sight of this dark, swift-moving current, but a great exultation lifts me up, affirms the deep wish that is in me never to leave this land"—an idyllic, pastoral vision that recurs at the end of the book (p. 61).

In the middle five episodes, Miller elaborates on his essential themes, linking the profane and the sacred, the obscene and the beautiful, in surrealistic passages that are unrivaled in American literature. Alone at a concert, Miller enters into an astonishing dadaistic reverie with images such as these:

It's as though I had no clothes on and every pore of my body was a window and all the windows open and the light flooding my gizzards. I can feel the light curving under the vault of my ribs and my ribs hang there over a hollow nave trembling with reverberations. How long this lasts I have no idea; I have lost all sense of time and place. After what seems like an eternity there follows an interval of semiconsciousness balanced by such a calm that I feel a great lake inside me, a lake of iridescent sheen, cool as jelly; and over this lake, rising in great swooping spirals, there emerge flocks of birds of passage with long slim legs and brilliant plumage. Flock after flock surge up from the cool, still surface of the lake and, passing under my clavicles, lose themselves in the white sea of space. And then slowly, very slowly, as if an old woman in a white cap were going the rounds of my body, slowly the windows are closed and my organs drop back into place. (p. 68)

Later, while taking a young Hindu to a whorehouse in Paris, Miller is again overcome by a cosmic vision prompted by a most concrete observation. This suggests an ethical basis by which Miller can conduct his life—namely, to accept the hopelessness of life, to expect nothing, to live life savagely. "If to live is the paramount thing," he concludes, "then I will live, even if I must become a cannibal" (p. 89).

The tenth episode, beginning on July the Fourth, concludes with the hero contemplating a return to America, but rejecting it again for Paris.

The final series of episodes begins with the fall rains. Miller moves in with Fillmore (Osborn). By Christmas he has accepted a dismal teaching post in Dijon, rendered as a nightmare with belly laughs. Here, as elsewhere, Miller proves himself a master of the vernacular, a Mark Twain from the alleys of Brooklyn. *Tropic of Cancer* is a humorous book, its satire bitter but salty and broad, in no way subtle.

The last episode completes the cycle of the seasons and everything begins anew. "It was spring before I managed to escape from the penitentiary," Miller announces as he returns to Paris (p. 260). Fillmore, the victim of what Miller terms a "typical Anglo-Saxon crisis," defined as "an eruption of morals," is trying to evade the clutches of a young French woman, and Miller assists him as he boards a steamer for New York City (p. 265). He has a vision of "the whole city spread out, from Harlem to the Battery, the streets choked with ants, the elevated rushing by, the theaters emptying" (p. 286). It is a vision of a mechanical life he rejects. In Paris, "where the river gently winds through the girdle of hills," a great calmness overtakes Miller; the Seine, he rhapsodizes, "is always there, quiet and unobtrusive, like a great artery running through the human body" (p. 286). In the end, this recurring symbol of the flow of life—the principle of the cyclic structure of the book—also becomes embodied in the narrator:

The sun is setting. I feel this river flowing through me—its past, its ancient soil, the changing climate. The hills gently girdle it about: its course is fixed. (p. 287)

Tropic of Cancer is not so much a novel—not even a roman à clef—as it is a new species of autobiography, a personal narrative composed in eclectic manner, true to the life Miller imagined he lived as he lived it. Certainly Miller the writer altered, exaggerated, and "fictionalized" the events and persons he met in Paris between 1930 and 1932; yet the Henry Miller in *Tropic of Cancer* is the same man the author felt himself to be in reality. Furthermore, the letters, diaries, and memoirs of Nin, Perlès, Bald, Lowenfels, Putnam, Fraenkel, Kahane, and others confirm that the literary hero had a literal source.

In 1931 Michael Fraenkel advised Miller to abandon the conventional novel, to begin fresh, to write as he lived day by day. It was advice Miller was already giving himself, and he would soon rearrange and embroider his firsthand experience in response to the imaginative truth it revealed. *Tropic of Cancer* is not a complete or literal record, but it is an essentially accurate and powerful account of Miller's life in exile. Fraenkel later observed of Miller:

The very manner of his life, the way he had to live it day by day, never sure of a roof over his head, never knowing where his next meal would come from or the next bit of change, the hectic uncertainty and tension all this produced—something which would have broken and rendered inarticulate and frustrate almost any other man—only made and appointed him. It gave the style of the *Tropic of Cancer* its deep, terrible immediacy, its dynamism, its tension, its desperate swing and beat. [13]

At the same time, *Tropic of Cancer* possessed a transcendental vision, at an opposite extreme but arising directly from the raw, dark experience of reality. For most of his life, Miller had been drawn from the chaos of his life and its thwarted desires to fiction, to art; in Paris he not only wrote a book, he wrote himself into a book. The impulse was transcendental. Miller's literary predecessor, author of a transcendent song of the self a century earlier, was of course Walt Whitman, and at its deepest level *Tropic of Cancer* was the dark mirror-image of "Song of Myself."

Although Edmund Wilson would soon hail *Tropic of Cancer* as "the epitaph for the whole generation of American writers and artists that migrated to Paris after the war,"[14] the book did not make Miller more than a few dollars until 1961, when it was lawfully published in America. By then *Tropic of Cancer* had achieved social and historical importance, not only as the last major subject of literary censorship in the West, but as a seminal document in early twentieth-century expatriate writing. As Samuel Putnam observed, Miller "summed up for us as no one else has the expatriates' Paris of the second phase; and I think it may be said that the *Tropic of Cancer* is to that phase what *The Sun Also Rises* is to the preceding one."[15]

Stylistically, *Tropic of Cancer* had a deep influence on the next generation of American writers as well, but not everyone praised Miller's work—even his best work. Czeslaw Milosz, for example, finds that Miller is too far outside the humanistic tradition and too absolute in his denouncements of an intellectual culture. Miller is a "plebian incarnation" of the trained-scholar Nietzsche, Milosz argues:

The mind, so weighed down with scholarly formulations that it is intimidated, cowed, and does not trust itself, is certainly a plague, and Miller's volcanic roar, indifferent to all authority, is fascinating, exciting, and like a Martian who has come across Earth's arts and sciences, he is sometimes dazzling in the freshness of his judgements. But his great writing talent masks the immature confusion in his mind.[16]

Kate Millett and other feminist critics have also dismissed Miller's sexual politics; Frank Kermode has disparaged Miller's narratives as lacking *mesure*; and many

critics have tended to relegate *Tropic of Cancer* to the
pile of interesting but second-rate and derivative "novels" in the American tradition.[17] Harry Levin, who testi-
fied in favor of publication of *Tropic of Cancer* before
the U.S. Supreme Court, later characterized Miller's
work as "an amusing but crude burlesque of Lawrence."
He granted Miller's "undeniable talent," gusto, and story-
telling skill, but felt that "unfortunately, and increasingly in his other work," Miller's "authentic vein of pun-
gent humor is adulterated by messianic rhapsodies—
Leaves of Grass gone to seed—which prove rather em-
barrassing."[18] Likewise, others praised Miller's power
but judged him a minor literary figure. His writings after
he left Paris proved his talent was meager. Had he ever
been the equal of James Joyce?

Those who believed that Miller was a major figure
agreed that he was not the equal of the monumental
Joyce. They admitted that his first work, *Tropic of Cancer*, was his best. Still, Miller was not to be dismissed.
They agreed with Norman Mailer's observation that
Tropic of Cancer "is one of the ten or twenty great novels
of our century, a revolution in style and consciousness
equal to *The Sun Also Rises*. You cannot pass through the
first twenty pages without knowing that a literary wonder
is taking place—nobody has ever written in just this way
before. . . . A time and a place have come to focus in a
writer's voice."[19]

Certainly Miller's life and art, his actual and imagined experiences, merged in Paris. There he could chronicle in a new, vital autobiographical form the story of a
lost generation which, grown weary of its dreams, now
wakened to a world in violent disintegration. The decay
of a culture nourished him. By 1934 Miller had achieved
the intentions he stated in a letter to Anaïs Nin two years
earlier. Then he had questioned whether "all this personal narration" was justifiable and whether the bold content would not stir up intense antagonism. He answered

his doubts by insisting on telling the entire truth of his experience without imposing any limits, swearing "not to leave out anything because of principles, art, or whatever it may be that has constrained men heretofore." Writing in the first person allowed him to achieve the intensely personal and *human* rather than *fictional* truth of experience the novel form ordinarily permitted.[20] *Tropic of Cancer* was a human testament. It was shocking in its time, and it exceeded many of the previous limits in modern literature. *Tropic of Cancer* was, finally, a monumental success. But caught in a worldwide embargo, it reached far too few buyers to secure financial independence for its author. Sales amounted to only a few hundred copies a year. The first phase of Henry Miller's expatriation closed on a triumphant note, but Anaïs Nin continued to pay the rent.

3

Paris:
Surrealism on the Seine

The publication of *Tropic of Cancer* in 1934 marked a personal and artistic triumph for Henry Miller, but he still could not earn a living in Paris. His marginal existence was temporarily suspended at the end of the year, however, when he joined Anaïs Nin and Otto Rank, her psychoanalyst, in New York City. Rank had set up a lucrative practice; Nin and Miller became associates. By the spring of 1935, Miller was seeing four patients a day, although he lacked any professional training. He was earning a good living for the first time in ten years, but on other fronts he was failing. He had hoped to marry Anaïs, especially after his divorce from June by proxy in Mexico City (December 20, 1934), but their relationship was not progressing. Moreover, Miller was unable to find American publishers willing to take a chance on his literary work. He did strike up a lasting friendship with writer William Saroyan, but among major American publishers, only Alfred and Blanche Knopf were sympathetic, and they did not choose to take on the American censors. After a promising start, Miller discovered that his fortunes in New York City had not improved. Nevertheless, when Nin returned to her husband in Paris in May, Miller stayed until he exhausted his resources. He returned to Paris in October 1935, broke as usual.

He brought with him, however, two slight books that were immediately published in Paris. Both were epistolary in form, growing out of two long letters Miller wrote to promote his literary standing. "No form, clearly, was closer to Miller's imagination than the letter," Jay Martin remarks. "The best of his writing always resembled the casual flow of an epistle to a familiar old friend interested in all his secrets."[1] The epistle was another autobiographical form in which Miller would record, as no other writer had, the essential narrative of an individual, modern artist.

The first published epistle, *What Are You Going to Do about Alf?* (1935), was an outlandish plea to readers to support Alfred Perlès (Alf) in his attempts to be a fulltime author. Miller admits that Alf once helped him survive as an artist in Paris; he now intends to return the favor:

What Alf did for me in his small way I am going to do for Alf now in a large way. I'm going to see that Alf gets to Ibiza and that he lives there like a prince until his book is finished.

For those who are too tired to read further I now give the important dope:

Send your checks, by the week or by the month, to me, Henry Miller, 18 Villa Seurat, Paris (14me). Keep firing until we say *Stop!*

(Notice: The cost of printing and distributing this letter which, out of delicacy, we have limited to 3,000 copies, has been underwritten by Michael Fraenkel and Eduardo Sanchez whom we hereby thank publicly and privately.)[2]

A second letter, *Aller Retour New York* (1935) was written to Perlès and was a deliberate attempt to write the longest published epistle in history. It incorporated Miller's impressions as an expatriate artist returning to the "sterile" and hostile native American soil. Miller argued that only the artist could redeem a culture that was being demolished by the heartless machineries of modern industrialism, bureaucracy, and Big Business.

At the same time, Miller "was drawn into what was probably the most elaborate scheme of artistic collaboration in the twentieth century," yet another epistolary excursion.[3] With Michael Fraenkel and, occasionally, Alfred Perlès, Miller began an exchange of letters upon the general theme of death, with Shakespeare's *Hamlet* as the initial focus. The correspondence would run until exactly one thousand pages were written—not a word more or less—and then be published verbatim, without editorial change. The intent of *Hamlet*, as Miller's biographer succinctly summed it up, was to create "a kind of artists' cathedral, a vast outline of the themes, plots, myths, fables, fictions, and characters which future artists would employ."[4] This notion, and much of *Hamlet*, published by Fraenkel's own press in two separate volumes (1939, 1941), was pretentious and finally boring. It did not always represent Miller's finest efforts as an epistolary artist, although as a project it suggests the experimental and unbounded creative energies Miller unleashed during the remainder of his stay in Paris.

It was also in 1935 that Miller finished a book of more serious note, *Black Spring*, which was sometimes as daring and dazzling as *Tropic of Cancer*. Miller later regarded it as his best effort at self-portraiture.

Black Spring is a series of ten sketches, what Miller called "Self-Portraits," based on three sources: reminiscences of his youth in New York, portions of his life in Paris excluded from *Tropic of Cancer*, and compositions in dadaistic and surrealistic style drawn from Miller's dreams, which he had been recording for several years at Nin's insistence. The unifying term in what is otherwise a miscellany of intense, unrelated pieces is "Self-Portrait." Miller was once again looking for a new way to write about himself. In *Black Spring* he "was bent not on giving his readers slices of life," as Jay Martin notes, "but his own life sliced into transparent cubist pieces—a self seen now this way, now that, a self existing only in its multiplicity."[5] Early in the actual writing of *Black Spring*, Miller told Nin he hoped he could succeed in his purpose "of putting down that large irrational area, of grappling with the unseizable . . . of proceeding multilaterally in all directions." He likened the structure to the "disoriented" design of a rag carpet.[6] It has been argued that *Black Spring* has a deeper continuity as well —that it is a funeral oration delivered in the blackest of seasons by a self that lives only by keeping in motion, sliding from one extreme to the next, dying in the throes of each experience and reborn in the next. All the contradictory impulses are welded together in an apocalyptic pastiche.[7] Certainly one sees the influence of Joyce, Lawrence, and Eliot in *Black Spring*, but not the structural unity of these writers. The fragments of Miller's self-portrait do not often cohere, as they do in *Tropic of Cancer*. Nevertheless, the separate episodes show us some of Miller's best work, both in the surrealistic and traditional narrative modes.

In the first two episodes of *Black Spring*, "The Fourteenth Ward" and "The Third or Fourth Day of Spring," Miller plunges into his origins, evoking his golden childhood days in Brooklyn. The Fourteenth Ward is the open street where "once you were free, wild, murderous."[8] It is an Eden, but an Eden with warts, rendered in stark, precise detail with a touch of surreal imagery:

> Where others remember of their youth a beautiful garden, a fond mother, a sojourn at the seashore, I remember, with a vividness as if it were etched in acid, the grim soot-covered walls and chimneys of the tin factory opposite us and the bright, circular pieces of tin that were strewn in the street, some bright and gleaming, others rusted, dull, copperish, leaving a stain on the fingers; I remember the ironworks where the red furnace glowed and men walked toward the glowing pit with huge shovels in their hands, while outside were the shallow wooden forms like coffins with rods through them on which you scraped your shins or broke your neck. (p. 5)

Childhood in the streets forms the deepest portion not only of Miller's memory, but of his being, and in later life it becomes one extreme in his definition of the essential self:

In youth we were whole and the terror and pain of the world penetrated us through and through. There was no sharp separation between joy and sorrow: they fused into one, as our waking life fuses with dream and sleep. We rose one being in the morning and at night we went down into an ocean, drowned out completely, clutching the stars and the fever of the day. (p. 9)

Repeatedly, Miller discovers that he can never be whole again, that he must live in fragments, but the fragments themselves serve as the elements of an extended rhapsody, a dadaistic eulogy rendered in Joycean style for the sensuous world of childhood. The second episode begins even earlier, in the house where Miller was born, but the images of his origins are now linked to his immediate circumstances in Paris, which he contrasts with his native land. He sees America as "spreading disaster," as "a black curse upon the world" (p. 21). He sees himself as a Whitmanesque artist in a dark century. "I regard myself not as a book, a record, a document, but as a history of our time," Miller declares. Then, contradicting himself slightly, he adds, "For me the book is the man and my book is the man I am, the confused man, the negligent man, the reckless man, the lusty, obscene, boisterous, thoughtful, scrupulous, lying, diabolically truthful man that I am" (p. 21). He is writing the book being read, and thereby creating himself at a feverish pace because he feels the end of the human world nearing. His thoughts sputter. "My faltering and groping, my search for any and every means of expression, is a sort of divine stuttering," Miller insists. *I am dazzled by the glorious collapse of the world!*"(p. 21). As before,

Miller concludes with a lengthy, sustained dadaistic passage, a burlesque of astrology among other things.

The third episode, "A Saturday Afternoon," is one of Miller's finest Paris rambles, interlaced with his celebrated comic tour of the best urinals in the city. The title comes to stand for Whitmanesque perfection—the day of unending sensual connection between man and divine nature. The lowest animal functions prompt high metaphysical excursions. "A Saturday Afternoon" is followed by Miller's description of the creative process in "The Angel Is My Watermark," a rather too obvious narrative of how the artist came to paint a watercolor "masterpiece." Miller does capture the associational way in which the Romantic, surrealistic artist proceeds, and as a painter he seems to prefigure the artists of the action school.

The episode at the center of *Black Spring*, "The Tailor Shop," has received the widest praise from critics. It is the most traditional narrative in the book, a fond and detailed account of the years Miller worked in his father's shop. There is little dadaism, but much portraiture. Miller also proves himself to be a superb raconteur. The theme is Miller's realization that his family is mad, and by extension the whole family tree of mankind is diseased; the tailor shop comes to stand for a dark, disintegrating world:

There is the morning world, which starts from scratch each day, and the busheling room in which things are endlessly altered and repaired. And thus it is with my life through which there runs the sewer of night. All through the night I hear the goose irons hissing as they kiss the wet seams; the rinds of the old universe fall on the floor and the stench of them is sour as vinegar. (p. 101)

Miller likens the world he hates to the busheling room of his father's tailor shop, a world of "endless alterations and repairs," but "never a new suit of clothes." It is a world he rejects, a world he believes is destroying itself. "The Tailor Shop" is an expression of Miller's early failure and bitterness, and it is a self-portrait in cruelty. The self is a reflection of an inhuman, murderous world in which it is trapped.

The final pieces of *Black Spring* are largely experimental in form and language. "Jabberwhorl Cronstadt" is a dadaistic dervish of sense and nonsense, a portrait of the nonstop talker, Walter Lowenfels, who befriended Miller in Paris. "Into the Night Life" is Miller's most completely surreal composition, a patchwork of his actual dreams, captured in the language of dreams, complete with the abrupt transitions and irrational landscapes of the unconscious. Miller begins by waking up in the midst of a nightmare, traveling the streets of an unreal Brooklyn, crossing deserts, exploring Coney Island after dark, and from there through a wild park to the street of his earliest sorrows, down into the depths of pre-Columbian America, and finally back home, a long and jolting journey through the depths of his consciousness. There is no plot, character, or structure in the traditional sense. It is pure surrealism. More comprehensible but also surrealistic is the next section, "Walking Up and Down in China," in which China stands for dreams, for escape from America, for a realm of pure being. The theme is the repeated deaths of the self and the rebirths that follow. Miller travels from America to Paris, then back to America (replete with a two-page list of people, places, and products in America), into the Fourteenth Ward, and finally to the end of the world, where a black spring seems to prevent a lasting rebirth.

Black Spring concludes with two humorous, dadaistic burlesques. Targets include Christianity, show business, and literary criticism. "*Black Spring* is full of parodies and puns, zany free associations and digressions, anarchy and irreverence," George Wickes notes. "Miller in a comic mood is constantly running off the

rails."[9] Indeed, Miller's energy is high and his imagery
unbridled in *Black Spring*. "The essence of the book was
its insistence on rambles, excursions, walks," Jay Martin
argues. "Miller pictured himself strolling through Paris,
through his past, through continents, through his
dreams, his roving mind, the seasons—toward the pos-
session of a new territory and a renewed consciousness."[10]

Some readers, however, found *Black Spring* the
self-indulgent work of a confused writer, too removed
from actual experience. *Tropic of Cancer*, for all its surrealism, anarchy, and exposition of grand ideas, was an-
chored in concrete experience, and that was the source
of its power. *Black Spring* was more abstract. Kingsley
Widmer felt that *Black Spring* was self-consciously "literary," forced rather than forceful. Miller had retreated
from the celebration and acceptance of reality in his first
book into a highly stylized language-world in his second
effort, and the result was, at best, a "weakly satisfying
anthology of rhetorical gestures."[11] There is some justice in this criticism. *Black Spring* is the execution of
certain aesthetic and philosophical ideas in which words,
images, and fragmented literary structures are primary,
while the experience of the self in the world is secondary. This proportion left many readers cold. Even Miller
sensed the danger when he wrote to Nin:

> I notice that I seem to revolve like that—from life, or ex-
> perience, to expression or art. . . .
> I feel I am coming out again into art. I think the ideas now
> take the place of experience in giving me the stimulus for
> expression.
> Is it awfully bad? That's what I wonder.[12]

Whether bad or not, Miller was able to write in the surrealistic and dadaistic veins as none of his American contemporaries was able or even inclined to do. Miller for-
mulated his own version of surrealism, and he was the

first major writer to introduce the technique successfully into autobiography.

In a formal sense, Miller was as much a dadaist as a surrealist. His dada masterpiece, in the opinion of several critics, is *Money and How It Gets That Way*, a sixty-four page pamphlet published by the author in Paris in September 1938.[13] It was prompted by a postcard from Ezra Pound, praising *Tropic of Cancer*:

> Great deal more to the book than I thought yester/after reading about 40 pages. NEVERTHELESS, though you realize the force of money AS destiny, the one question you haven't asked yourself is:
> What IS money?
> who makes it/how does it get that way?///[14]

Pound was obsessed with economic theories at the time, especially with the idea of Social Credit, but Miller was not so serious about world finance. *Money and How It Gets That Way* is pedantic nonsense "written in such impeccable jargon that economists have been known to take it seriously."[15] An amusing mock treatise surveying the history of money, it examines finance in endless tautological detail and becomes a source book of academic gobbledygook:

Whatever it may have been in the past, money has come to be what it now is only through thinking about it. Money has no life of its own except as money. . . . A primitive Bantu, for example, would never have made the mistake of confounding the object of barter with the act of bartering itself. On the other hand, the highly civilized Greeks of Pericles' day were often guilty of such absurd substitutions, due perhaps, we should say in all fairness, to the exaggerated role which logic played in all their forms of speculation.[16]

What Miller admired in surrealistic art, as in the paintings of Georges de Chirico, was a lack of harmony and balance, the intensity of each element autonomously and unconsciously arranged in chaos, and the dissolution of logic and convention—all primarily elements of dada. Miller was an early admirer of Bunuel and Dali's surrealistic cinema, but he praised the antics of dada's founder, Tristan Tzara. Dadaism encouraged humor, disorder, and destruction in literature, elements Miller had already discovered in himself and learned to express as soon as he left America.

In "An Open Letter to Surrealists Everywhere," first published in 1938, Miller discusses the use and meaning, but not the techniques, of surrealism. Surreal art is grounded in "what is active, immediate, and personal"; it is a means to "destroy the barriers" and to "revive the primitive, anarchic instincts." The surrealist is concerned primarily with himself and his own experience. He is opposed to all social and cultural restraints. The surrealist enters the unconscious and discovers "embryonic spawn of the coming angels, demons, and madonnas" that illuminate the "dim relationship between the bankruptcy of the conscious intellectual forces . . . and the emergence of this new great empire of darkness." The unconscious, Miller concludes, "in its demand to be explored and charted, will revive the sensory powers of man so that he may look upon the world about him with renewed exaltation and more vivid consciousness."[17] In fact what Miller is describing is as much American transcendentalism as it is European surrealism, more a philosophy than a literary technique or aesthetic program.

This essay on surrealism, like others Miller wrote to explain himself in the thirties, was itself another form of autobiography—the personal essay—and is a document in twentieth-century individualism, a continuation of Thoreau's "Life without Principle," Emerson's *Representative Men*, Whitman's "Democratic Vistas." In Miller's view, surrealistic art was almost any art that concerned the individual's struggle to transcend the confines of his society or culture. This did not mean Miller could not write more strictly defined surrealistic prose, for he did so in *Tropic of Cancer*, *Black Spring*, and exhaustively so in shorter pieces such as *Scenario (A Film with Sound)*, first published as a separate volume by Obelisk Press in 1937.[18]

As its title indicates, *Scenario* is a screenplay. There is no dialogue. It is a series of surrealistic landscapes and events, divided into nine parts, made coherent by its repeated imagery and the continuity of its two female characters, Alraune and Mandra. *Scenario* is modeled on Anaïs Nin's first novel, *House of Incest* (1936), which Miller had a hand in publishing. The Alraune character in *Scenario* was based on June Miller, the Mandra character on Anaïs herself, and Miller's screen version of Nin's prose fantasy was his attempt to understand the buried psychological forces at work in 1932 when Henry, June, and Anaïs were locked in a passionate triangle. The intensity of *Scenario* is created by its extraordinary imagery and its violent transitions. The themes of love and death are explored through repeated clashes of associated imagery—fire, smoke, volcanoes, the moon; bone, desert, sand, surf. Miller appears in his script as the Astrologer, entranced with Mandra (Anaïs), but unable to release her from the sensual spell cast by the protean figure of Alraune (June).

Both Miller's essay on surrealism and his scenario based on *House of Incest* were included in his finest essay collection, *Max and the White Phagocytes*, issued by Obelisk Press in 1938. Together with *Black Spring*, this volume represents Miller's most important work outside of his longer personal narratives such as *Tropic of Cancer*, *Tropic of Capricorn*, *The Colossus of Maroussi*, and *The Rosy Crucifixion*. *Black Spring* had been a series of shorter narratives, surrealistic, dadaistic, and natural-

istic in form; *Max and the White Phagocytes* was the re-
pository of miscellaneous film reviews, essays, letters,
and narrative portraits.

Max opens with a portrait of Miller's friend, Hans
Reichel, a German painter who became one of the Villa
Seurat circle that gathered around Miller in Paris after
1934. Titled "The Cosmological Eye," this essay is also
one of Miller's many statements on the effect and the
plight of the Romantic artist in an unromantic century.
"Glittering Pie," the next essay, is extracted from *Aller
Retour New York*, Miller's account of his unsatisfactory
return to America in 1935. This is followed by film reviews of work by Gustav Machaty ("Reflections on 'Ex-
tasy'") and Luis Bunuel ("The Golden Age"). Miller saw
L'Age d'Or at Studio 28 shortly after arriving in Paris and
had been stunned by its use of surrealism. That film by
Bunuel and Salvador Dali had convinced him that cinema could become a major art form. The techniques of
cinematic surrealism would play a significant role in
Miller's own literary art.

"Un Être Étoilique" is a review of and homage to
the diaries of Anaïs Nin; Miller was probably the first
critic to read Nin's diaries in their entirety. "Via Dieppe-
Newhaven" is a comic narrative of Miller's thwarted attempt to visit England. "The Universe of Death" is extracted from the mass confusion of Miller's aborted study
of D. H. Lawrence and forms a coherent statement of
how Miller differed from the literary giants of his
time—from Joyce, Proust, and Lawrence. To this collection Miller also attaches one of his finest letters, part
of the earlier "Hamlet" correspondence with Michael
Fraenkel. Like many of the essays in *Max*, it is both a
self-portrait of the artist and an analysis of modern art.
The inseparability of the artist from his art is clearly at
the heart of Miller's aesthetic vision.

The title piece of *Max and the White Phagocytes* is a
narrative of Miller's encounters with Max Bickel, a Jew-

ish-American tailor living in Paris. Max is a pathetic, impoverished, and neurotic figure with whom Miller has much in common, and he is treated with a mixture of sympathy and scorn in one of Miller's most successful and moving narratives:

I began to accept him as a natural phenomenon: he was a part of the general landscape, like rocks, trees, urinals, brothels, meat markets, flower stalls, and so on. There are thousands of men like Max roaming the streets, but Max was the personification of all. He was Unemployment, he was Hunger, he was Misery, he was Woe, he was Despair, he was Defeat, he was Humiliation. . . . Everything he said was true, horribly true. . . . People don't want to hear these truths. They *can't* hear them, for the reason that they're all talking to themselves in the same way. The only difference is that Max said them aloud, and saying them aloud he made them seem objective, as though he, Max, were only the instrument to reveal the naked truth.[19]

Miller has lived the same "horrible truths" and transcended his sufferings in Paris, but Max "had become suffering itself," and Miller is able to portray him in as powerful a manner as he portrayed his other acquaintances in *Tropic of Cancer*, a book that "Max" closely resembles.

Max and the White Phagocytes can be read as an explication of *Black Spring*. Portions of both were collected in *The Cosmological Eye*, the first book by Henry Miller to be published in America. The publisher, James Laughlin, was the founder of New Directions, which would publish more of Miller in America than any other press. As an undergraduate at Harvard, Laughlin had attempted to reprint the first ten pages of *Aller Retour New York* in the *Harvard Advocate* (1935), but police seized and destroyed the first press run and briefly jailed the editors. Laughlin included the banned excerpt, titled "Glittering Pie," in *The Cosmological Eye*. In his *New Direction* annuals of 1936 and 1937, Laughlin also introduced Americans to edited passages from *Black Spring*. In *The Cosmological Eye* (1939), he included the original contents (somewhat expurgated) of *Max and the White Phagocytes*, shortened the "Hamlet" letter, and then added three pieces from *Black Spring* ("Jabberwhorl Cronstadt," "Into the Night Life," and "The Tailor Shop"), an essay on Paris ("Peace! It's Wonderful!"), an extended "Autobiographical Note" by the author—one of the most succinct and frank résumés Miller ever composed—and a summary essay entitled "The Brooklyn Bridge."

"The Brooklyn Bridge" repays our attention as much as any essay Miller wrote in his Paris years. It is both a key to the bewildering themes of *Black Spring*—it would have served that book well as a coda—and a literary bridge between Miller's life in America and later exile in Paris. Miller begins by praising the labyrinth of the modern metropolis where, in the midst of anarchy and confusion, he feels at home. It is homeward in a metaphysical as well as a literal sense that he is drawn "for inspiration and nourishment." Later, memory and the "prophetic, troubling dreams" of maturity become indistinguishable from the waking state, a condition he renders surrealistically in his Paris writings. Miller explains the "violent dreams and visions which accompanied the writing of *Black Spring*" by making reference to his image of the Brooklyn Bridge. The bridge represents a link to the past and a force destroying his early illusions, ideals, and hopes. "It enabled me to link the two ancestral streams which were circulating between the poles of death and lunacy," Miller wrote. "Henceforth I could plant one foot firmly in China and the other in Mexico." Miller's divided ancestry, his divided self, receives many names in *Black Spring*; China and Mexico were just two. China suggests a transcendent, peaceful state; Mexico suggests a sensuous, violent state. The two states are in conflict in

Miller, joined peacefully only on rare occasions when the literal and imagined bridge becomes "the harp of death, the strange winged creature without an eye which held me suspended between the two shores." In America, Miller portrays himself as "the North American thug," a heartless creature in internal dissolution. "That is why, in studying the air-conditioned quality of the American nightmare, I am enchanted by the prospect of re-arranging the debris which has accumulated on the shores of that isolated island of incest," Miller explains. "The man of to-day is being carried along on the face of his own flood; his most wakeful moments are no different in quality or texture from the stuff of dreams." Thus Miller justifies his fascination with a past he would like to cast off, but to which he is bound by birth: as an artist, he wants to alter the debris of the past, creating a meaningful, transcendent experience. "His life is the foaming crest of a long tidal wave which is about to smash on the shores of an unknown continent," Miller writes prophetically of the individual today. "He has swept his own debris before him; he will break clean in one steady accumulated wave." Crossing Brooklyn Bridge, Miller has a transcendent but far darker view of America than Walt Whitman did from Brooklyn Ferry.

Finally, Miller looks from *Black Spring* to the future:

The book which I speak of was a sort of musical notation in alphabetical language of a new realm of consciousness which I am only now beginning to explore. Since then I have crossed the Equator. . . . The whole southern hemisphere lies exposed, waiting to be charted.[20]

Black Spring serves as this bridge between the *Tropic of Cancer* and the *Tropic of Capricorn*, between present and past, life and death, Paris and America.

In Paris, Miller created the three autobiographical forms—fictive, expository, and epistolary—which he

would continue to fill in over four more decades. Increasingly, he would turn back to America, finally able
to capture himself and the meaning of his life there from
the perspective of Paris. He had learned and achieved
far more than anyone, himself included, would have predicted. It is difficult to refute the claim that Henry
Miller is "one of the important writers of his time, one of
the most expressive of the Thirties, and certainly the
best surrealist writer America has produced."[21]

In the "Autobiographical Note" concluding his first
American book, Miller summed up the literary credo he
had been formulating in *Black Spring* and *The Cosmological Eye*. He declared he was not a realist, a natural-
ist, a political writer, or a pornographer, but a writer interested in the personal life of the individual, which he
sought to render through anarchy, myth, and dream.
He also adopted an anti-art position for the first time,
insisting, "Ninety-nine percent of what is written—
and this goes for all our art products—should be destroyed."[22]

4

**Paris:
End of an Era**

Ever since 1922, when Miller wrote the first abysmal draft of his adventures as employment manager for Western Union Telegraph Company, he had been trying to write the story of his life in New York City. On May 21, 1927, while employed as a gravedigger for Queens County Park Commission, he set down twenty-six pages of notes outlining an epic novel on that subject. The same day, Lindbergh completed a solo flight from New York to Paris, a monumental accomplishment that made Miller feel his failure more sharply. Only after Miller made his own New York to Paris journey, near the end of his expatriation, was he finally able to write the book he had begun seventeen years earlier. It would be his last major book in Paris.

Miller had been writing and abandoning versions of *Tropic of Capricorn* since 1932. After reading Peter Abelard's famous autobiography of misfortunes in 1936, Miller began again. By 1938 he had a definitive draft. In a letter to Anaïs Nin, he spelled out the significance of the titles of his first and last Paris books, drawing a contrast between them:

For me Cancer means the Crab, as it was known to the Chinese sages—the creature which could move in any direction. It is the sign in the Zodiac for the poet—the halfway station in the round of realization, which changes when one comes to the constellation Libra. Opposite Cancer in the Zodiac (extremes of the Equinox—turning points) is Capricorn, the house in which I am born, which is religious and represents renaissance in death. . . .[1]

Cancer was a portrait of death-in-life, but its hero was very much alive. In *Capricorn* the hero was swallowed by death, living only to escape. *Cancer* celebrated personal liberation; *Capricorn* condemned the imprisonment of the self in its house of birth, New York.

Tropic of Capricorn opens with a grim self-portrait. Henry Miller is a less than admirable character living in the midst of chaos, confusion, and discord. He is indifferent to those around him and extremely stubborn:

From the very beginning I must have trained myself not to want anything too badly. From the very beginning I was independent, in a false way. I had need of nobody because I wanted to be free, free to do and to give only as my whims dictated. The moment anything was expected or demanded of me I balked. That was the form my independence took. I was corrupt, in other words, corrupt from the start.[2]

Miller then turns on his family, criticizing them as unimaginative—strict Nordic immigrants content to become the petite bourgeoisie of America. "They were painfully clean," Miller complains. "But inwardly they stank. Never once had they opened the door which leads to the soul; never once did they dream of taking a blind leap into the dark" (p. 11). From a more objective viewpoint, Miller admits that his criticisms were actually self-directed:

In my bitterness I often search for reasons to condemn them, the better to condemn myself. For I am like them too, in many ways. For a long while I thought I had escaped, but as time goes on I see that I am no better, that I am even a little worse, because I saw more clearly than they ever did and yet remained powerless to alter my life. (p. 11)

Miller's aim is to alter himself, but he is a product of his own past and a victim of his present environment. This

self-portrait in bitterness is also a condemnation of society, but ultimately it is not America that Miller blames.
The responsibility for self-liberation, for beginning the
metaphysical journey into the self—the "one great
adventure"—is Miller's own.

Whenever Miller condemns America, he condemns
himself. "The whole continent is a nightmare producing
the greatest misery of the greatest number," Miller
writes, but he goes on to chronicle how he spread that
misery himself (p. 12). It is only when Miller learns to
reach inward that he finds meaning apart from America.
Ultimately, that meaning is in art, in the act of writing
which is self-creation, "in this which I am doing now,"
Miller declares, "something which is parallel to life, of it
at the same time, and beyond it" (p. 13). By rejecting
America, Miller finds himself as an autobiographical artist. As he creates himself in his art, he runs parallel to his
actual life, recording it, and transcending it, wrenching a
pattern of meaning out of the chaos. We can read this autobiography in a double way, just as the author writes it
in a double way—as the chronicle of a life and as a meditation on its meaning.

After introducing himself as he was in America,
Miller recounts the story of how in an act of desperation
he became Employment Manager at the Park Place office of Western Union Telegraph Company (1920)—
here called the Sunset Place office of the Cosmodemonic
Telegraph Company of North America. "In a few months
I was sitting at Sunset Place hiring and firing like a de-
mon," Miller writes. "It was a slaughterhouse, so help
me God. The thing was senseless from the bottom up"
(p. 19). In short, the Telegraph Company is a symbol of
American inhumanity and heartless organization.

It is the effect of American institutions on individuals that Miller now looks into, presenting a series of anecdotes portraying the desperate lives of the messengers
he hired. The result is a deliberate, savage reversal of

the Horatio Alger myth in which honest, hard work is
supposed to be rewarded by success and happiness. "I
will give you the picture of twelve little men, zeros without decimals, ciphers, digits, the twelve uncrushable
worms who are hollowing out the base of your rotten ed-
ifice," Miller declares. "I will give you Horatio Alger as
he looks the day after the Apocalypse, when all the stink
has cleared away" (p. 31). Parallel to the stories of these
messengers is the process of artistic creation. Miller recalls that his attempt to write about the nightmarish
melting pot of messengers resulted in "the worst book
any man has ever written" (p. 34). Miller was not yet the
artist in fact that he was in desire. To become an autobiographical artist, Miller had to rid himself of the false
American selves he had acquired. He had to destroy
himself to become his genuine self. "You have to be
wiped out as a human being in order to be born again as
an individual," Miller writes. "You have to be carbon-
ized and mineralized in order to work upwards from the
last common denominator of the self" (p. 35). Having
completed this process in Paris, Miller can now write
the book of the messengers that he could not write in
1922. "Most of us live the greater part of our lives submerged," Miller observes. "Certainly in my own case I
can say that not until I left America did I emerge above
the surface. Perhaps America had nothing to do with it,
but the fact remains that I did not open my eyes wide
and full and clear until I struck Paris. And perhaps that
was only because I had renounced America, renounced
my past" (p. 49). In a literal sense, *Tropic of Capricorn*
renounces America on nearly every page, but of course
Miller is also reclaiming his past in the very process of
recreating it. There is a negative energy that he taps as
he evokes the bitter past.

The narrative that runs through *Tropic of Capricorn* is anecdotal. Episodes range from Miller's adventures as a child to his indiscriminate sexual encounters as

an adult. Many of these anecdotes are exaggerated, and the humor can be that of the street, of the burlesque house, or of the "unique Dadaist in America," as Miller entitles himself (p. 286). The Telegraph Company sequences and the portraits of Miller's father, sister, and eccentric acquaintances are all part of a dark vein of satire that Miller introduces into twentieth-century autobiography. This vein originated in the native comic tradition associated with Mark Twain. His pen warmed in hell, Miller like Twain carves his way out of "siviliza-tion"; unlike Twain, Miller does not make a tragic return to society because Miller's vernacular hero is transcendent. His boyish street humor punctuates a genteel, hypocritical society not with the brilliant wit Twain exhibited, but with crude intensity. For this twentieth-century Huck Finn, the whorehouses and sewers of Paris are the exile's raft and river. The whole North American continent is the shoreline of corruption and enslavement. Miller is writing obscene letters to earth, celebrating an adolescent sexual freedom, thumbing his nose at an inhuman culture. He has inherited from Twain that vernacular tradition, based on regional humor (the lower-class Brooklyn of Miller's birth), that as literary art converts serious issues into double-edged comedy—"an inversion which implies the conventions yet remains their opposite."[3] Conventional values are seen as a form of slavery for the self. The comic inversion of conventional morality is an escape from tyranny, a flight toward personal freedom.

Institutions, however, are not the ultimate enslaver; the individual conscience, which incorporates the social order, is the real culprit. For Huck and for Henry, the conscience is "an agent of aggression—aggression against the self or against another," either the "means or the excuse by which pain is inflicted . . . erasing the possibility of choice and thereby constraining its victims to a necessary and irrecoverable course of action."[4] Miller

makes himself the vernacular hero in order to discover a
road to freedom, outside society, outside his own conscience. In *Tropic of Capricorn*, Miller is still trapped by
his American conscience, but the deeper story is of his
struggle to destroy what is destroying that deeper self.

Humor serves a spiritual purpose as well. "When
the whole human race is rocking with laughter," Miller
insists, "laughing so hard it hurts, I mean, everybody
then has his foot on the path" (p. 304). Laughter dis-
solves the normal distinctions and restrictions imposed
by society. In this dissolution, the genuine self is revealed as transcendent.

The violence of rebirth, although constantly
thwarted in the narrative of *Tropic of Capricorn*, is always present as Miller's guiding desire. "I want to pass
beyond the responsibility of fatherhood to the irrespon-
sibility of the anarchic man who cannot be coerced nor
wheedled nor cajoled nor bribed nor traduced. . . . Even
if I must become a wild and natural park," Miller declares, echoing an image from *Black Spring*, "inhabited
only by idle dreamers I must not stop to rest here in the
ordered fatuity of responsible, adult life" (p. 145). As
America's finest literary anarchist since Thoreau, Miller
preaches the politics of extreme personal freedom, often
in passages of dadaistic satire, as when he imagines the
nation under his anarchical Presidency (pp. 281–82).

Throughout the book Miller is presented with a vast
gulf between his vision of personal liberation and his imprisonment in the mechanical reality of America. He has
glimpses of a richer world beyond Brooklyn and of a better self, of the artist he might become, but he is powerless to change. Above all, he is caught up in what he
terms "the sex and death chant" (p. 93). Sex and death,
two basic themes in American literature, are central
themes in *Tropic of Capricorn*, and they are symbiotic.
Sexuality is death-in-life. It receives its most intense

treatment in the Ovarian Trolley and Land of Fuck sequences—the surrealistic heart of the book. The uterine world of unrestricted sexuality is at the root of human existence, but it is as formless, as chaotic, as the oppressive world of American society. Therefore Miller employs his descriptions of sexuality, both the naturalistic and surrealistic versions interlaced throughout *Tropic of Capricorn*, as a means to reject and combat a repressive outer world. In an effort to transcend Brooklyn and the ordinary, everyday self he has become, Miller will invert sexual values, overthrow taboos, expose moral hypocrisy, and even attempt to trace the sexual impulse to its hidden source. Nevertheless, Miller finds that sexual activity is not an end in itself and at a deeper level not a certain means to spiritual transformation. Whether on the Ovarian Trolley, in the Land of Fuck, or in the "real" world of casual (usually exaggerated) sexual encounters, Miller escapes society and himself only temporarily, if at all. It is still death-in-life at all levels, with only a few hints that something revitalizing exists elsewhere. Miller has mastered the language of death, but he cannot turn it against death itself. He cannot build a new language that "cuts through the death language of the day like wireless through a storm" (p. 290).

Still, the language that denies life is ideal to create the deathly portraits that populate *Tropic of Capricorn* and produce some of Miller's best passages. His portrait in black of Broadway can scarcely be surpassed:

Broadway, such as I see it now and have seen it for twenty-five years, is a ramp that was conceived by St. Thomas Aquinas while he was yet in the womb. It was meant originally to be used only by snakes and lizards, by the horned toad and the red heron, but when the great Spanish Armada was sunk the human kind wriggled out of the ketch and slopped over, creating by a sort of foul, ignominious squirm and wiggle the

cuntlike cleft that runs from the Battery south to the golf links
north through the dead and wormy center of Manhattan island.
(p. 98)

Yet Miller yearns most for the language of life. Broadway
is rendered as a world of death from which he seeks
liberation.

The liberating event that unifies the apparently
aimless anecdotes and extravagant surreal effusions of
Tropic of Capricorn and brings order and meaning to
the deliberate chaos of Miller's self-portrait in America is
his meeting with June at a dance hall in 1923. It has been
implicit throughout the book—primarily in the position
of the narrator who stands outside the drama he creates,
on the other side of the liberation he once desired but
could not reach. "I like to dwell on this period when
things were taking shape," Miller announces in the middle of his confusion (p. 177). He is recreating the source
of his unlikely liberation, the source of his desire to become more than he had been, more than an urban
drifter, a Brooklyn boy. *Tropic of Capricorn* is a modern
Divine Comedy in autobiographical form. Civilization is
Miller's Inferno, sexuality his Purgatoria, and the liberated imagination his Paradiso.[5] When he meets June,
Miller says, "I am born anew, born and baptized by my
right name: Gottlieb Leberecht Müller!" (p. 228). With
June he finds the strength to escape the Inferno of the
Telegraph Company. The sexual Purgatoria of his past
becomes a Paradiso of the senses and the new realm of
the artist. The hero of the narrative and the author of the
narrative become one.[6] "At the point from which this
book is written," Miller declares, "I am the man who
baptized himself anew" (p. 230).

It is the moment of Miller's transformation, his liberation from the past, and his discovery of life. But all
this has a coda. If June (Mona) helped Miller escape his

old life, there was still the new relationship to face. Love
proves to be another, more intense version of death-in-
life.[7] Even love is insufficient, and the relationship
eventually collapses. What endures in its stead is art.
Only Miller's birth as an artist satisfies his longings to be
free, to become himself. Visiting the exact spot in New
York where he first met June, Miller tells us:

It came over me, as I stood there, that I wasn't thinking of her
any more; I was thinking of this book which I am writing, and
the book had become more important to me than her, than all
that had happened to us. (p. 333)

This was not a realization Miller wanted to accept;
rather, it was forced upon him. *Tropic of Capricorn* is
dedicated to HER, to June, but it is as Miller concluded
"a tomb in which to bury her—and the me which had
belonged to her" (p. 334). The act of self-creation is what
endures, what transcends "the frame of personal misfor-
tune" and brings happiness in the place of misery.

   Tropic of Capricorn is more concerned with the
birth of the artist than with the rebirth of the man. "The
intensity of the relationship with Mona brought life and
new hope," William Gordon notes, "but the sexual world
they shared prevented his development as an artist. In
order to complete his development, he had to convert
experience into art."[8] That experience was largely negative, but Miller could scarcely ignore his past in
America. As an exhaustive autobiographical artist, he
was driven to give a full account of himself not only in
multiple literary forms (fictive, expository, epistolary),
but from multiple points in time. Gradually Miller was
achieving continuity in his canon. If the order of composition is reversed, it is clear that the negative image of
the self in *Capricorn*, immersed in the dissolving fluids
of *Black Spring*, becomes the positive image of the self
in the intense light of *Cancer*. The particular failures of

the twenties created the successes of the thirties; the story of the self was the story of reversals, of deaths and rebirths.

For Miller, *Tropic of Capricorn* represented a transition "from consciousness of self to consciousness of purpose," but it was only the prelude to a fuller account of his life in New York.[9] *Tropic of Capricorn* did mark the end, however, of seven years of brilliant writing in Paris. His odyssey would next take him to Greece, and shortly to America, where he was destined to return in fact as he already had in his fiction. In *Tropic of Capricorn* Miller had reached the negative extreme of the Dionysian life he had celebrated in *Tropic of Cancer*. It now remained for him to discover his equator, a way between and beyond his tropics.

5

⚡⚡⚡⚡⚡⚡⚡⚡⚡⚡⚡⚡⚡⚡⚡⚡⚡⚡⚡⚡⚡⚡⚡⚡

Greece:
Voyage into Light

The publication of *Tropic of Capricorn* brought the Paris decade to a close. As the shadow of an impending German invasion darkened the continent, Miller was deciding how to evacuate. In April 1939, he wrote Anaïs Nin:

By the time you get this we'll probably know whether there's to be a war or not. It's difficult to think about anything else. Everybody is excited or depressed. Am waiting for Hitler's famous speech tonight. The whole world sits and waits to hear what one man says—it strikes me as thoroughly ridiculous.[1]

A few weeks later, Miller was selling those of his belongings he couldn't pack. "Such a running around—never did so much in my life," he told Anaïs. "Glad to get out of Villa Seurat—what a swamp of details!"[2] On the last day of May 1939, Miller departed from Paris. In his initialed valise, he placed souvenirs: a salad fork, a thimble, an ashtray.

His literary expatriation had ended, symbolically if not literally. For the next few months, he would travel in France, staying in Rocamadour, Nice, and other cities, until reaching Marseille. On July 18, 1939, he boarded the *Théophile Gautier* and sailed for Greece.

Waiting there on the island of Corfu was Lawrence Durrell. Henry Miller's relationship with Lawrence Durrell ranked second only to that with Anaïs Nin. In August 1935, Durrell, a twenty-three-year-old aspiring writer, wrote a fan letter to forty-three-year-old Miller, praising *Tropic of Cancer*. Miller immediately replied, "You're the first Britisher who's written me an intelligent letter about the book. For that matter, you're the first anybody who's hit the nail on the head."[3] Durrell and Miller were soon exchanging manuscripts and hatching plots to increase the circulation of Miller's banned books. Their immense correspondence would chronicle the second half of Miller's expatriation in Paris.

In September 1937, Durrell finally visited Paris, staying upstairs at 18, Villa Seurat. In December, Miller launched the "Villa Seurat Library," which would include Miller's *Max and the White Phagocytes*, Anaïs Nin's *Winter of Artifice*, and Durrell's *Black Book*. The project was printed by Obelisk Press and paid for by Durrell's wife, Nancy. The Villa Seurat Library strongly resembled Miller's "Siana Series," published by Obelisk in 1935 with Anaïs Nin as underwriter. (The books then were Miller's *Aller Retour New York*, Nin's *House of Incest*, and Richard Thoma's *Tragedy in Blue*.) Durrell arrived in Paris during Miller's best years. A literary circle had developed with 18, Villa Seurat as its center, and Durrell became an energetic member before returning to Greece in 1938.

Durrell had tried for months to convince Miller that Corfu was an ideal spot to weather out the Nazi storm threatening France, but Miller was considering another destination. "I wish I could say that I would see you in Greece soon," Miller wrote Durrell as late as April 1939, "but I turn towards America, towards the desert particularly. I want so much to see it again, the waste places, the grandiose, the empty spots, where man is nil and where silence reigns."[4] Weeks later, however, Miller chose the escape route to Corfu. It was to be the first stop on a worldwide tour:

My itinerary is roughly as follows with allowances for change, if climate etc. is no good for me: Corfu, Monaco, Athens, Istanbul, Dalmatia, Belgrade, Sofia, Bucharest, Vienna, Warsaw, Paris, London, Devonshire, Cornwall, Wales, Dublin, Killarney, America via New Orleans. . . . Then to Bagdad, Teheran, Jerusalem, Bethlehem, Egypt, Fez, Timbuctoo, Singapore, Java, Borneo, Bali, Easter Island, Siam, Indo-China, Rangoon, Ceylon, the whole Indian continent, Darjeeling, China, Tibet—punkt![5]

It was an impossible itinerary, especially with the world at war, but Miller made his first destination, arriving in July 1939, at the village of Kalami, Corfu.

In Paris, Miller was able to write first about his immediate circumstances in exile, then about his past in America. In Greece he was again swept up by the immediacy of a new world. Paris had once corresponded with the inward forces that Miller expressed in the savage surrealism of *Tropic of Cancer*, but as the exotic became familiar, Miller turned from Paris to America—from the present to the past—for literary stimulus. It was not until he reached Greece at the end of the decade that he would again find the inner and outer forces in perfect alignment. The result was *The Colossus of Maroussi*, an account of Miller's tour of Greece.

Much more contemplative in content and tone than *Tropic of Cancer*, *The Colossus of Maroussi* does not express the discovery of the self as artist. Instead, the artist discovers a greater self. In *Tropic of Capricorn* Miller had written that his deepest desire was not to live, "but to express myself."[6] Autobiographical art was then parallel to life, and superior to it; but in Greece art and autobiography seemed less important than the metaphysical forces they expressed. It was nature and spirit, not society and sensuality, that concerned Miller now. *The Colossus of Maroussi* records a quest for "pure vision," for a primitive form of consciousness in which myth and life were united.

In a long letter to Anaïs Nin written in Paris on February 21, 1939, Miller foreshadowed the new nature of his quest. He had come to an understanding of desire, will, and selfhood similar to that of the Zen masters.[7] He now declared that art was no longer of the essence. "We must drop the pen, the pencil, the brush and become the whale itself," Miller declares. "The real experience lies yonder in the deep waters. . . ."[8] Appropriately Miller is swallowed by Greece. He makes no show of resistance. Unembittered, he relaxes his quarrel with America, with history and society. Receptive to a new landscape, he plunges into the depths of myth and the individual psyche. He does not quite "drop the pen," however. He continues the saga of himself, finishing another major chapter in a single stroke. "The fact is that in Greece Miller completes the second cycle of his life, begun in Paris, which proved as rich as the earlier cycle in Brooklyn had proved barren," Ihab Hassan has observed. "The land itself, mythic and real, allows him to see his life whole, and to unseal his lips in benediction."[9]

Miller prefaces his voyage into "a world of light" with an account of the Dordogne valley in France, which he visited just before embarking for Greece. His description sets the stage by contrast—this "black, mysterious" region of northern Europe precedes his flight "into the bright and hoary world" of the Mediterranean—but both the Cro-Magnons of Dordogne and the ancient Minoans and Greeks possessed a primitive, sacred vision of life that "will live on just as dreams live on and nourish the souls of men."[10] Miller boards his ship on July 14, 1939, and arrives at Piraeus on July 19. He visits Athens, but only the blistering heat leaves an impression. "There is nothing inviting about it," Miller initially reports.

"There is something not only arid and desolate about the scene, but something terrifying too. You feel stripped and plundered, almost annihilated" (p. 8). On his first evening in Greece, however, Miller makes contact with an elemental existence:

The dust, the heat, the poverty, the bareness, the contained-ness of the people, and the water everywhere in little tumblers standing between the quiet, peaceful couples, gave me the feeling that there was something holy about the place, some-thing nourishing and sustaining. (p. 11)

Leaving Athens by boat to meet Durrell at Corfu, Miller becomes more entranced with that elemental world he glimpses outside European history:

There was no time any more, just me drifting along in a slow boat ready to meet all comers and take whatever came along. Out of the sea, as if Homer himself had arranged it for me, the islands bobbed up lonely, deserted, mysterious in the fading light. I couldn't ask for more, nor did I want anything more. I had everything a man could desire, and I knew it. (p. 13)

Pulling into the port of Patras, he enters a "new realm as a new man" (p. 14). Greece is the "sacred precinct" of war-ravaged Europe and of Miller's own quest for peace.

With the Durrells, Miller settles into the simple life, living closer to nature than ever before, even taking a week's camping trip on an isolated bay of Corfu; but his idyll is interrupted when the Greek army is mobilized. Miller accompanies the Durrells to Athens to gauge the situation. There he meets George Katsimbalis, a Greek version of Blaise Cendrars and a monologist without equal. "He talked about himself because he himself was the most interesting person he knew," Miller comments. "I like that quality very much—I have a little of it my-self" (p. 28). The passionate figure of this storyteller be-comes an emblem of the anarchic Greek spirit:

On the high verandah in Amaroussion, just as the light from the other worlds began to shed its brilliance, I caught the old and the new Greece in their soft translucence and thus they remain in my memory. I realized at that moment that there is no old or new, only Greece, a world conceived and created in perpetuity. The man who was talking had ceased to be of human size or proportions but had become a Colossus whose silhouette swooned backwards and forwards with the deep droning rhythm of his drug-laden phrases. (p. 40)

It is also in Athens that Miller discovers a new aspect of himself, locked in the ruins and released by the light. On the Sacred Way to Eleusis he feels the effect of this light on the remains of a pre-Christian culture: "Here the light penetrates directly to the soul, opens the doors and windows of the heart, makes one naked, exposed, isolated in a metaphysical bliss which makes everything clear without being known" (p. 45). This transfiguring force is manifest everywhere, and the self must learn to absorb it.

Now Miller's journey is from one illumination to the next, gathering in intensity. Miller passes through the Straits of Poros as through the womb. At Hydra he loses "all sense of earthly direction" and begins his journey through the natural and mythological landscape of Greece. Each station of this "voyage into the light" marks a new aspect of Miller's spiritual self-awareness.

At Epidaurus, on what Miller calls the "road to creation," he reaches an understanding of himself that rivals in intensity his discovery of himself as an artist in Paris. He feels healed after thirty years of conflict with the world and with himself. Here he declares that "all conquest is vain, even the conquest of self, which is the last act of egotism" (p. 80).

The next station lies at the opposite pole—Mycenae, a Cyclopean world of primeval terror. Epidaurus had been "a bowl from which to drink the pure spirit: the blue of the sky is in it and the stars and the winged creatures who fly between, scattering song and melody," but Mycenae "folds in on itself, like a fresh-cut navel, drag-

ging its glory down into the bowels of the earth where
the bats and the lizards feed upon it gloatingly" (p. 88).
Miller feels himself slipping back into a dark pit where
"even the light, which falls upon it with merciless clar-
ity, gets sucked in, shunted off, grayed, beribboned"
(p. 88). It is a savage world of monstrous crimes. Blood
and violence are the rule. Parting with Katsimbalis,
Miller refuses to descend the staircase into "that slimy
well of horrors" (p. 91). He turns back toward the light,
unwilling to penetrate the darkest depths below. Having
experienced natural bliss, he refuses to descend into the
realm of primitive chaos.

In the second part of the book, Miller journeys to
Crete. At Phaestos, which he identifies with the female
principle in Minoan civilization, he experiences a moment of cosmic unity:

This is the first day of my life, said I to myself, that I have included everybody and everything on this earth in one thought.
I bless the world, every inch of it, every living atom, and it is
all alive, breathing like myself, and conscious through and
through. (p. 161)

This is Henry Miller's version of Walt Whitman's *Passage to India,* a series of poems expressing a cosmic journey of the soul.

In the concluding episodes, Miller returns to
Athens. He takes solitary, peaceful walks: "Somewhere
beyond the 'ammonia' region, in a forlorn district whose
streets are named after the philosophers, I would stum-
ble about in a silence so intense and so velvety at the
same time that it seemed as if the atmosphere were full
of powdered stars whose light made an inaudible noise"
(p. 181). He makes an excursion to Delphi, across the
plain of Thebes where there is "a terrific synchronization
of dream and reality, the two worlds merging in a bowl
of pure light, and we the voyagers suspended, as it were,
over the earthly life" (pp. 188–189). Katsimbalis be-

comes the modern oracle of Delphi, and Miller once
more is able to transform his thoughts of death and violence into celebrations of life and peace.

The final destination is again Mycenae. He returns
with the Durrells on Christmas Day, 1939, descends the
staircase into the well of darkness, and stops as before:

I experienced the same feeling of terror as I had the first time
with Katsimbalis, more, if anything, since we had descended
deeper into the bowels of the earth. I had two distinct
fears—one, that the slender buttress at the head of the stairs
would give way and leave us to smother to death in utter darkness, and two, that a mis-step would send me slithering down
into the pit amidst a spawn of snakes, lizards, and bats. (p. 215)

When Durrell decides to turn back, Miller admits he
would rather die than be forced to descend any farther.
The Colossus is a book of light, not of darkness, of peace
in a world of war. The book ends as Miller stands in Aga-
memnon's tomb, a "citizen of the world . . . dedicated to
the recovery of the divinity of man" (p. 241). In Greece,
Miller completed the liberation of the self he had begun
in Paris. He was ready to return to his native land:

The prospect no longer filled me with dread. Greece had done
something for me which New York, nay, even America itself,
could never destroy. Greece had made me whole and free.
(p. 210)

Greece also provided Miller with new aesthetic
principles that he applied to the composition of *The Colossus of Maroussi*. The stark simplicity and individual-
ity of the landscape were reflected in the plain, colloquial narrative, and light became the central theme. "I
suddenly realized that the universe is nothing but light,
light, light!" he told Anaïs Nin in a letter from Corfu.[11]
The very geology had become a projection of Miller's inner unity, his resolution of Dionysian and Apollonian
forces. "Only here have I understood the meaning of na-

ture," Miller wrote.[12] Nature is the mirror of the transcendent human spirit.

Whole and free, Miller boards the *Exochorda* for the long voyage home on December 27, 1939. He has just turned forty-eight. In *The Colossus of Maroussi* he declares that he "shall pass from art to life, to exemplify whatever I have mastered through art by my living" (pp. 205–206). Art has initiated the self into a new way of life, but the ultimate goal is complete liberation, even from art. "To continue writing beyond the point of self-realization seems futile and arresting," Miller concludes. "The mastery of any form of expression should lead inevitably to the final expression—mastery of life" (p. 206).

As an aesthetic principle, this leads to silence, to the transcendence of art, but the autobiographical impulse was so strong in Miller he would never abandon art altogether. Bound for America, he realizes that what has happened to him in Greece will vanish "into the well of experience" and the "incredible light of Attica" will dim unless he can now make the passage from life to art.[13]

The result of this observation is *The Colossus of Maroussi*, Miller's finest autobiographical entry since *Tropic of Cancer*. It is a book of extremes and extravagances—of spiritual excesses. Each episode leads to a more intense moment of transcendence. *Tropic of Cancer* was at the opposite extreme, an account of the self in which each episode led to a more intense celebration of the senses. Both books capture the immediacy of extreme experiences. Both employ extravagant literary devices. *Tropic of Cancer* is a surrealistic autobiography without rival, except for Whitman's *Leaves of Grass*; *The Colossus of Maroussi* is a personal narrative of a sojourn into transcendent nature. Its closest parallel is Thoreau's *Walden*.

While in Greece, Miller wrote that his intent was "to pass beyond the sphere and influence of art."[14] At

the same time, however, he suggests that he is a new
kind of artist who can never finish writing:

Even now I do not consider myself a writer, in the ordinary
sense of the word. I am a man telling the story of his life, a process which appears more and more inexhaustible as I go on.[15]

6

~~~~~~

America:
The Way Home

In January 1940, Henry Miller returned to New York City. His decade of savings amounted to ten dollars, exactly the amount Emil Schnellock had staked him to when he left for Paris ten years earlier. None of his major books could be published in America; he would have to wait another twenty years before the U.S. Supreme Court lifted the ban on *Tropic of Cancer*, as well as many other works that followed. "In the fifteen years which had elapsed since I began my career I had not only proved incapable of supporting myself by my efforts," Miller admitted, "but I had substantially increased my debts. . . . All I had to my credit were a few books which more than likely will never be published in this country, at least not as they were written." Miller wrote these lines of confession in an account of his homecoming, "Reunion in Brooklyn."[1]

In retrospect, Miller dubbed his return to New York "one of the worst periods in my life," but "Reunion in Brooklyn" would be the finest personal essay he would write in the forties—"truthful to a fault," as Miller later observed.[2] In the narrative, Miller tells of his dread at seeing his family. The bitter associations had not been transcended even in Greece. He avoids the ordeal of homecoming for weeks. Then when he first catches sight of his father, who is terminally ill, he "feels like a criminal, like a murderer" (p. 98). He breaks down

and weeps, filled with compassion for his family and re-
morse for abandoning them; their house is "like a pol-
ished mausoleum in which their misery and suffering
had been kept brightly burning" for the prodigal son's
return (p. 99). The evening's conversation is painfully ordinary, a portrait of suffering and sorrow without exaggeration or drama. The father who is dying has become a
good-hearted, tolerant fellow. The mother means well
and sacrifices continually, although she is too tight with
money and still ashamed that Henry is not working a "respectable" job. Nevertheless, Henry looks forward to
these family visits. He is able to assuage his guilt by
helping out, bringing presents, and looking after his in-
valid father.

The essay ends when Miller attends a party with all
his relatives in the "house which my grandfather had
bought when he came to America" (p. 127). Anxious to
have a look at the Fourteenth Ward, he sneaks outside
in search of a street he remembered from boyhood and
later dreamed about in Paris. The old reality and the
dream begin "to fuse and form a composite living truth"
as Miller walks the old neighborhood. Finally he comes
upon a "street which corresponded exactly with that
ideal street which, in my dream wanderings, I had
vainly tried to find." It lies "beyond the frontier of my
childhood explorations," Miller reports; it is an other-
worldly street located in Paradise. In fact, this place
where there is a "miraculous accord between desire and
reality" is an ordinary neighborhood of families "gathered in a circle, smiling good-naturedly as they con-
versed with one another, their bodies relaxed, their
spirit open and expansive." It is this simple, harmonious
vision of communal life, this small circle "which is the
whole goal of life," that had never been Miller's to share
(pp. 128–129). It is the idealized reversal of his actual
family reunion. No real reunion is possible for Miller in
Brooklyn except in the Brooklyn of his dreams. As

Kingsley Widmer first observed, when Miller is con-
fronted with the bitter abundance and inner emptiness
of America, he escapes "into the subject of his writing,
the romance of the memory which attempts to remold
the past with some now lost significance."[3] Based on the
plain facts of "Reunion in Brooklyn," however, such an
escape is not entirely irresponsible. For the rest of his
life Miller would be deeply concerned with working out
his complex and violent relationship to America. His art
would be a way of not only expressing, but discovering,
the essence of that relationship. He had not wished to
return. He preferred Paris, he much preferred
Greece—or so he would always protest. As he admitted
in "Reunion in Brooklyn," however, he still had to come
to terms with the old wounds. "Deep down, I suppose,
was the realization," Miller wrote, "that I had left something unfinished in America" (p. 97).

Coming to terms with America required making a living,
as Miller knew all too well. He tried writing pornography at a dollar a page, but found the task deadening.[4]
Two deliberately obscene pieces, written for a private
patron, eventually merged as *Quiet Days in Clichy,* an
energetic narrative of carefree Paris adventures—a
lesser companion to *Tropic of Cancer.*[5] "Reflections on
Writing," the essay he had composed in Greece, led to a
longer meditation, a full statement on Miller's intent and
his use of sexuality in art, published openly in Paris and
privately in America as *The World of Sex.*[6] Miller also
completed the manuscript of his illumination in Greece,
but he was unable to sell it. Finally he hit upon a scheme
the publishers bought. It followed a thoroughly American plan: armed with an advance, he would tour the
country and write about his impressions. He had described just such a book to Jack Kahane of Obelisk Press
years earlier, and in August 1940 he signed a contract.
Doubleday supplied a $750 advance. Henry bought a

1932 Buick, learned to drive, and set out on October 26 to survey America. After a year's tour, he gathered his impressions into a book of essays, *The Air-Conditioned Nightmare* (1945).

Despite his denouncements of his native land, Miller set out with some hope of discovering a Whitmanian America, worthy of a song of joy such as he had sung for Greece. He wrote the log of his journey on the printer's dummy of an edition of Whitman's *Leaves of Grass,* but he could not celebrate the continent as the Romantics of the nineteenth century had. This was not surprising. Months before, he had complained to Anaïs Nin:

I'm afraid of the monotony everywhere, the uniformity, the lackluster life or lifelessness. I begin to wonder if it's any use knocking about the land—though it may be unfair to judge the whole by the little I've seen. The *land* is all right—it's the people—the bleak absence of anything vital or meaningful. That eats into one quickly. One would have to be a Colossus to withstand it.[7]

The actual journey would confirm Miller's fears, and his written account would lack energy and focus. *The Air-Conditioned Nightmare* was no *Colossus*. Miller's ambivalence and confusion about America diluted his literary efforts. He was at his best when he was positive, when he was obsessed with the vision of a place, as he had been in Paris and Athens. America was still his nightmare.

Miller's letters to Anaïs Nin are often more interesting than the miscellaneous essays that make up *The Air-Conditioned Nightmare*. Driving out of the Holland Tunnel—"like coming out of a great intestine"—Miller headed for Washington, D.C.[8] He spent several weeks in Virginia (where Emil Schnellock was teaching), then headed south. He interrupted this swing to attend his parents' wedding anniversary in New York and returned to Asheville, North Carolina, in December, meeting the ex-convict he portrayed in a chapter of *The Air-Conditioned Nightmare* ("The Soul of Anaesthesia"). By January 1941 he had driven no further than Jacksonville, Florida, where he found "the uprooted lost souls of America milling around in a rabbit stew," much as he had fifteen years earlier.[9] By the end of January, he had met the seventy-year-old painter and surgeon, Dr. Souchon, and toured the grounds of Weeks Hall's mansion, "The Shadows," in New Iberia, Louisiana. Both encounters are the bases of chapters in *The Air-Conditioned Nightmare*.

While in Natchez, Mississippi, Miller received word that his father was dying. Henry arrived on February 8, two hours too late. He stayed in New York until March 2, 1941, before heading out again, passing now through Pittsburgh, Cleveland, Detroit, and Chicago, until he again reached Natchez to reclaim his car. In April he headed for California via Santa Fe. In Albuquerque he wrote Nin:

I could tell that there would be nothing ten days after I started out. Only the scenery is compensating. Around here it is quite magnificent. The mountains are bare, rocky, scintillating —rising up to 12,000 feet and covered with snow. There are less than 500,000 people in the whole state. The best country is always where there are the least people.[10]

He acknowledged that it would have been better to accept America, but he was unable to do so.

In May, Miller left the Grand Canyon for Hollywood, a ride he described at the time as "epic" and "fantasmagorical!"[11] Hollywood itself was not so bad as he imagined; in fact, he stayed in the area that summer, writing about his American travels, and returned to New York on October 9.

Two days after his fiftieth birthday, a road-weary Henry Miller wrote to Lawrence Durrell in Cairo:

You know, I'm back from the tour. Covered about 25,000 miles. A year wasted, I'd say. Am bringing the book to a close soon. Now well over 500 pages. But I doubt that it will ever be published.[12]

Doubleday turned down the manuscript and Miller paid back his advance. By the time *The Air-Conditioned Nightmare* was published in 1945, most of its unrelated episodes had appeared in various magazines. The book was only of slight interest, lacking focus and stylistic force. The best chapter—symptomatic, perhaps, of the book's lack of inspiration—was "My Dream of Mobile," which was more concerned with Paris and the America of the imagination than with an actual city in Alabama.

In 1942 Miller returned to southern California, settling in Beverly Glen near the UCLA campus. He had hoped to work as a writer in Hollywood, but, as he told Durrell, "I have made no effort to get myself a job. I loathe the work and the people who run the show."[13] After six months he had earned one hundred dollars; he could not raise the fare to return to New York, the same problem he had in the early Paris era. The Big Sur period was about to begin, however, and for the rest of his life Miller would, for the most part, call California home.

In 1943 Miller made more money from painting than writing. For a few months his watercolors suddenly sold as fast as he could turn them out. Although he prospered, Miller soon concocted new schemes to ensure financial survival—schemes with a touch of boldfaced humor. One of his "open letters to all and sundry," begging for a loan, was circulated among friends and published as an advertisement in magazines. It read in part:

It gripes me that in a year when seventeen books of mine are being published, here and in England, I should be in this predicament. It is phenomenal to have that many books published in one year. It is even more phenomenal that the author of those seventeen volumes should be reduced to the ignominious position of a beggar. But that has been my lot always in this country. And that is why I want to flee it as soon as possible.[14]

While conceding that he had made some money unexpectedly as a painter, Miller insisted he had used it to pay back previous loans. "I was an optimist," he wrote, "and slightly delirious. Now I am being absolutely honest when I say that all I got out of this sudden influx of wealth was three pairs of woolen socks, a plaid woolen shirt, and some good water color paper." Miller estimated he still owed $24,000. "That is what it has cost me to write as I pleased for the last twenty years."[15] Or at least that was what it had cost others.

In truth, Miller was not wealthy; occasionally, he was destitute. In February 1944, he moved to Big Sur, finally settling there in a rent-free cabin on Partington Ridge. Big Sur represented a new beginning for Miller, especially in his attempt to establish peace between himself and America. It continued the transition he had begun in Greece—from the civilized to the primitive, from art to life, from the air-conditioned nightmare to a back-country monastery. He explained to his friends that he enjoyed living closer to nature, although the strenuous life terrified him. Still, the Big Sur country was irresistible:

Back from the coast, over the mountains, there is an absolute emptiness. It is almost as forbidding as Tibet, and it fascinates me. I should like to go back in there and live for a time quite alone.[16]

That desire for solitude ended abruptly. In July, Miller met a twenty-year-old Bryn Mawr graduate, Janina Martha Lepska. They were married on December 18, 1944, and lived at Big Sur. A daughter, Valentine, was born in 1945 and a son, Tony, in 1948. Miller doted on both his offspring. Big Sur was a native version of Greece, Miller's China of pure being. The outsider had finally come home.

Many of the books that appeared under Miller's name in the forties were collections of his essays, most of which

had been published earlier. These did not sell particularly well. If Miller was to make a living as a writer, it
would have to come from the interest in his banned
books, which were legally for sale only in France. In the
war years, Miller's books finally began to sell. On October 2, 1944, Maurice Girodias, son of Jack Kahane,
wrote from Paris that Miller was due $40,000 in royalties
from Obelisk Press—an incomprehensible sum to
Miller. The money could not be sent out of postwar
France, however, and by the time these restrictions
were relaxed, the franc was so devalued that Miller had
almost nothing to collect. In 1946 *Tropic of Cancer* and
Tropic of Capricorn were banned even in France, until
a committee which included André Breton, Albert
Camus, Paul Eluard, André Gide, and Jean-Paul Sartre
came to Miller's defense.

By the end of the decade, it was clear that Miller's
literary achievement in America had not begun to rival
that in Paris. He wrote less and often it was revision. Jay
Martin described Miller's apparent literary decline this
way:

He no longer felt the joy that had once given his writing vividness and verve. Now he grimly cranked out a steady succession
of works; but something in his imagination had relaxed, consol-
idated, ceased to go forward. Most of his work in the mid-to-
late forties emphasized the same ideas, had the same tone. He
wrote more quickly than ever before and usually contented
himself with one quick polish of a typescript. His style became
smoother—and more predictable. [17]

If a return to America had failed to inspire Miller
with an immediacy of place that he could transform into
a lasting and original work of art, he did produce one
book of importance by turning from actual circumstances
to more purely literary concerns. For years he had been
intrigued by the French poet Arthur Rimbaud. In California the critic Stuart Gilbert, who had translated some

of Rimbaud's poems, rekindled Miller's interest in the enfant terrible of French symbolist writers:

Anyway, about Rimbaud. I was in bed. I got excited, and then I came out with this—which I mean—that I place Rimbaud, as writer, above any writer I can think of. Meaning for what he attempted, for his purity and fidelity. I added that in some way I had gone off the track myself. That I wanted—that would be my ultimate aim—to get back to that quality which Rimbaud had and which distinguishes him, for me, from all other writers.[18]

This close identification prompted Miller to write an extended critical essay on Rimbaud, eventually published as *The Time of the Assassins*.[19] It was not, however, a book of literary criticism, but another species of autobiography written in the form of a critical study. The subject was again Henry Miller.

The Time of the Assassins begins more like the autobiography it is, giving the circumstances of its author's, not its subject's, life:

It was in 1927, in the sunken basement of a dingy house in Brooklyn, that I first heard Rimbaud's name mentioned. I was then 36 years old and in the depths of my own protracted Season in Hell. (p. 1)

Miller proceeds to draw the essential comparisons between himself and Rimbaud. At eighteen Rimbaud reached his great crisis, turning from literature to life; at thirty-six, the age at which Rimbaud dies, Miller passes through his own crisis, turning in the opposite direction, from life to literature:

Rimbaud restored literature to life; I have endeavored to restore life to literature. In both of us the confessional quality is strong, the moral and spiritual preoccupation uppermost. (p. 5)

The essential parallels Miller mentions are a love of the music of language, an "underlying primitive" nature, the urge to rebel, and the desire to become a new self, one at odds with the old world:

The new man will find himself only when the warfare between
the collectivity and the individual ceases. Then we shall see
the *human* type in its fullness and splendor. (p. 6)

This is a familiar theme in Miller's writing—a tired and
bombastic one when his writing is uninspired, as it was
in *The Air-Conditioned Nightmare*. In *The Time of the
Assassins*, however, Miller finds a new context and he
gives his themes and proclamations, as well as his self-
portrait, a fresh, revitalized treatment. With Rimbaud as
a point of comparison, Miller is able to describe and ana-
lyze his own desires, his own past, his own difficulties in
life and art.

As literary criticism, Miller's study of Rimbaud is
neither systematic nor illuminating. As a statement of
twentieth-century Romanticism, however, it has authority. When Miller emphasizes the demonic basis of modern Romanticism in relation to Rimbaud—its infantile
and destructive, as well as Dionysian, urges —he speaks
of his own art, too. Enlarging upon that definition, he
underscores the transcendental and pagan aspects. Art is
a means to destroy the old barrier between civilization
and individual desire, between discontent and ecstasy,
between Thanatos and Eros. Insofar as art becomes a
means to discover and express individual autonomy and
personal joy, however, it is antithetical to modern institutions. The art of Rimbaud, like the art of Henry
Miller, is an expression of revolt. What Miller sees in
Rimbaud is an inability to move beyond that revolt, to
return and accept life joyously, without rebelling but
also without confirming. Miller sees the limits of his own
art in Rimbaud's eventual bitterness and despair. He
hopes to take his writing in another direction, towards
metaphysical illumination as he did in *The Colossus of
Maroussi*. The danger that Miller does not recognize is
that the power of his art, born in rebellion, may be di-
minished by any kind of reconciliation with his demons.

Miller's study of Rimbaud can be dismissed as unscholarly and self-indulgent. This was the author's intention. For Miller, fiction, literary criticism, and philosophy were all of a piece, part of the fabric of the self. *The Time of the Assassins* was not so much an application of the pathetic fallacy to academic study as it was another form of autobiography. In America, Miller had not entirely lost the autobiographical impulse nor his desire to create new forms of self-expression. At Big Sur, moreover, he found what he had failed to find at his reunion in Brooklyn, a place, he wrote, "which deeply satisfies me, and which I thought unobtainable."[20] He told Nin that "what I am about to learn is simply the meaning of 'home,' the one thing I have never known. And when that finally becomes a part of me it won't matter where or how I live. That home in Brooklyn, which I always see when the word home is mentioned, is the insane asylum. That was never my home."[21]

Appearances and proclamations aside, Miller had not lost his serious literary ambitions at Big Sur. All during the forties, in fact, he had been engaged in a new personal narrative; its scale dwarfed even that of *Tropic of Cancer;* and it would be his last major effort to unite the fictional and confessional genres. He still believed he could surpass all his earlier achievements with an epic trilogy that would be franker, fuller, and closer to actual life than anything anyone else had written.

7

Brooklyn:
The One Great Story

The one great story Henry Miller promised himself to write was not about his exile in Paris in the thirties or his return to America in the forties, but about New York in the twenties, when expatriation was scarcely a dream. He had begun to tell this story in *Tropic of Capricorn* (1939), his last Paris work, but it would take twenty years and three more volumes to complete. Those three volumes—*Sexus* (1949), *Plexus* (1953), and *Nexus* (1960), the trilogy called *The Rosy Crucifixion*—provide an exhaustive chronicle of Miller's desperate struggle to find himself as an artist in Brooklyn. The crucial period is from 1923 to 1928 when he was married to his second wife, June, the most important woman in his autobiographies. *Tropic of Capricorn* had already covered the years 1920 to 1923, when Miller, married to his first wife, Beatrice, and father of one child, held a respectable position as employment manager for Western Union Telegraph Company. In *The Rosy Crucifixion* it is this life that crumbles, and from the ruins a new hero —the artist in rebellion—rises.

In composing an account of his rebirth in Brooklyn, Miller departed from the techniques that had served him so well in Paris. *Tropic of Capricorn* had been an experimental personal narrative in the vein of *Tropic of Cancer* and *Black Spring*—elaborately structured and highly surrealistic. *The Rosy Crucifixion* was simple and

direct. The surrealism was more muted, the tensions relaxed, the pyrotechnics muffled. The inventive lyricism
that had made Henry Miller perhaps the major literary
innovator of the thirties disappeared.

By sacrificing his lyrical energies in *The Rosy Crucifixion,* however, Miller effected an epic intensification of
the ordinary, the mundane, the inherently undramatic.
Many critics found the reading too ordinary. Ihab
Hassan dubbed this trilogy "perhaps the most tedious
achievement of our time."[1] Certainly this, Miller's
longest sustained narrative, almost sixteen hundred
pages in its American version, remains his most controversial major work. Much of the controversy concerns
whether *The Rosy Crucifixion* has any literary merit
whatsoever. At the very least, however, it captures a
time, a place, and a set of characters, through its unre-
lenting accumulation of detail and repetition, which has
a peculiar power—a power like that of an apparently artless but finally revelatory photograph album of the literal. Miller sets out to write yet another kind of autobiography, one that pushes "fictional" confession to the
limits of what is literary.

Sexus, the first volume, opens when Miller strays into
Wilson's Dance Hall on Broadway and there falls in love
with one of the hustling taxidancers, known first as
Mara, then as Mona. The entire trilogy follows the
events of Miller's actual life so transparently, however,
that it is obvious the Mona/Mara we read about is really
June Edith Smith Mansfield, Miller's second wife, who
will soon replace Beatrice (known as Maude in the narrative). It is the summer of 1923, and Miller's affair with
Mona and his divorce from Maude are the subjects of
Sexus, which will end with his marriage to Mona (June
1, 1924). "I was approaching my thirty-third year, the
age of Christ crucified," Miller notes. "A wholly new life
lay before me, had I the courage to risk all."[2] Miller is

desperate but not courageous. He is rebellious, but too unsure of himself to marshal his own rebellious forces. After meeting Mona, he simply allows events to run their course and thereby breaks one bond of society —that of marriage. His marriage, mean and loveless, had been an obstacle on the dim road to a new life. To become an artist means to reject the role of the responsible family man. The two were *not* compatible in Miller. Blaming Maude for his entrapment and unhappiness, Miller eventually discovers the fault is his own. By not knowing himself, by failing to act on his genuine desires (to become an artist and live outside society), Miller has not only made himself suffer; he has inflicted suffering on his wife and child. Burdened by this guilt, he is unable to abandon Maude. At the same time, he is unable to relinquish Mona, the woman who can lead him to a "wholly new life." He solves this dilemma by taking no decisive action, leaving the outcome up to chance.

If Miller is ambivalent about marriage, even when it restricts his development as an artist, he is more deliberately rebellious against the sexual proscriptions of his society. The frank, unbridled sexuality of *Sexus* emphasizes Miller's more general indictment of his culture and expresses his desire for complete autonomy. It is not sexual freedom he seeks, but the freedom to begin the new life that he has previously denied himself. The relationship between characters, as between individuals and a repressive moral code, is rendered in exaggerated sexual terms. The rampant sexual promiscuity of *Sexus* is ultimately an expression of the individual's desire to transcend the severely limited possibilities of urban industrialized life on all fronts. Sexual repression—and Miller's wild inversions of accepted sexual behavior—becomes merely symptomatic of larger, thoroughly inhuman forces at work in modern culture.

Yet once Miller is divorced from Maude and symbolically freed from one bond of society, he is not instan-

taneously reborn as the Romantic artist. He must cling
to his meaningless position at the Telegraph Company,
pay alimony and child support, and let Mona work
nights at the dance hall where she hustles other lonely
"admirers." Both Henry and Mona are sexually indiscriminate. They deceive each other about their affairs.
Nevertheless, Miller is utterly ensnared by Mona:

She is completely mine, almost slavishly so, but I do not possess her. It is I who am possessed. I am possessed by a love
such as was never offered me before—an engulfing love, a total love, a love of my very toe-nails and the dirt beneath
them—and yet my hands are forever fluttering, forever grasp-
ing and clutching, seizing nothing. (*Sexus,* p. 208)

Miller is not even on sure footing with his liberator and
protean muse.

The price of his illicit love is guilt. "We were feverish to begin a new life," Miller writes, "and we felt
guilty, both of us, for the crimes we had committed in
order to embark on the great adventure" (*Sexus,* p. 212).
One Sunday while Henry visits Maude and his daughter, Mona attempts suicide. This deliberately melodra-
matic act seems to atone for the sin of adultery.

Henry and Mona can then begin anew again. They
decide to move to another apartment, Mona quits her
dance hall job, and their relationship finally solidifies
when they are married before a Justice of the Peace and
two hired witnesses in Hoboken, New Jersey. Although
this shabby ceremony depresses them, it elicits the
finest sustained surrealistic passage in *Sexus,* a portrait
of a New York burlesque hall of the twenties without
equal in American literature (*Sexus,* pp. 588–614).

While *Sexus* is a faithful, drawn-out account of the
decisive year in which Miller ended his first marriage
and began his second, it is also a vivid tableau of character and anecdote. The characters are ordinary people
caught in the harsh circumstances of the period, drawn

from actual life. Like Miller himself, they are marginal types, desperate to break away but powerless to do so. Ulric (modeled on Miller's boyhood friend, Emil Schnellock) is a commercial artist who longs to depart from Brooklyn for the culturally more refined milieu of Paris. Stanley (modeled on another of Miller's early friends, Stanley Borowski) is a failed writer, a drunkard who revels in Miller's failures. Dr. Kronski (modeled on Emil Conason) is an anti-Romantic who sees death and futility in modern culture and, as such, becomes Miller's intellectual nemesis. MacGregor (modeled on two of Miller's earthiest cronies, Alec Considine and William Dewar) is a lower-class, comic foil—a hard-boiled Don Juan unhappy with his humdrum life but unwilling to change anything. MacGregor is Miller's mirror image, except that Miller now begins to break with his past and defy convention. As he puts the repressed but common desires of the individual into practice, he longs to escape from this Brooklyn gallery:

What I secretly longed for was to disentangle myself of all those lives which had woven themselves into the pattern of my own life and were making my destiny a part of theirs. To shake myself free of these accumulating experiences which were mine only by force of inertia required a violent effort. Now and then I lunged and tore at the net, but only to become more enmeshed. My liberation seemed to involve pain and suffering to those near and dear to me. Every move I made for my own private good brought about reproach and condemnation. I was a traitor a thousand times over. (*Sexus*, p. 262)

Only Mona urges Miller to follow his inner voice. She has always lived at one remove from actual life, from the sordid realities of her gold-digging profession. Even her dreams are fraudulent, borrowed from textbooks. "If she could fake her dream life, what about her waking life?" Miller wonders (*Sexus*, p. 337). Nevertheless, it is precisely Mona's ability to invent another reality that attracts Henry and inspires him to live out his own dreams. "Perhaps that mysterious quality of Mona's lay not in obscuration but in germination," Miller remarks (*Sexus*, p. 506). Inspired by Mona, Miller alters his reality. He begins to lead an anarchic, irresponsible life, the life of the Romantic, the life the others denounce but secretly envy.

Miller began writing *Sexus* shortly after his return to America in 1940. By 1942 he completed the first draft, but not until seven years later, after frequent revisions, did he send it to Paris for publication. Far more sexually explicit than *Tropic of Cancer*, *Sexus* was not likely to be published elsewhere. *Plexus*, the second volume, was written about the same time *Sexus* appeared (1949), but it was not published until 1953. The most striking difference in this second volume is a lack of sexual content. The central event in *Sexus* is sexual liberation—a rebellion against conventional morality and a discovery of the values of extreme personal freedom. The central event in *Plexus*, however, is economic. When Miller quits his job at the Telegraph Company, he severs his economic bond with society. In *Plexus* he and Mona begin their struggle for survival on the fringes of society. The relationships in the book are, accordingly, not sexual but economic and literary (for it is to become a full-time writer that Miller rejects conventional employment).

After November 1924, Mona must provide the income. She does so by fleecing a contingent of wealthy admirers, dazzling them nightly in Greenwich Village. While her "occupation" troubles Henry, he accepts it. He must sacrifice everything for art, he believes, but he is unable to write anything of value. "I was so in love with the idea of being a writer that I could scarcely write," Miller admits.[3] Convinced he had to write a novel in the mold of a Dreiser, a London, or a Joyce, he sees the source of his failure only in retrospect: "I was far too self-conscious, in the early days, to use my own voice" (*Plexus*, p. 58).

As his literary failures multiply, Miller's life becomes increasingly chaotic and marginal. Mona constantly changes jobs in the Village. The Millers frequently fall behind on the rent. At times they are reduced to begging on the streets. Both Henry and Mona are dreamers, destined to survive by the skin of their teeth when luck is with them, by the handouts of friends and family when their fortunes sour. Their life together in *Plexus* begins on a high note at 91 Remsen Street in a fashionable section of Brooklyn; it rapidly declines thereafter. At one point they open a small speakeasy in a basement apartment on Perry Street. Henry works as bartender and cook, and he must pretend to be Mona's employee so as not to scare off her free-spending gentlemen callers there. This venture, like all their others, is doomed. "To run a speakeasy, which is what we are doing, and to live in it at the same time," Miller notes, "is one of those fantastic ideas which only arise in the minds of thoroughly impractical individuals" (*Plexus*, p. 392).

Even more impractical is Miller's plan to cash in on the Florida land boom of 1925. Lured south by his old friend O'Mara (modeled on a longtime friend and adventurer, Joe O'Regan), Miller hitchhikes to Jacksonville on Thanksgiving and returns to New York by Christmas, destitute. The speakeasy meanwhile has folded. Henry and Mona must live apart, with their respective families, until Miller is commissioned to write an article for *Liberty Magazine* (an article which was never to appear). With this payment they can once again afford a place of their own. In July 1926 Miller is lured south a second time by promises of a quick fortune from O'Mara; the results are once more disastrous.

By the end of 1926, Mona has resumed her gold-digging ventures as a waitress at a Village nightclub and

Henry is attempting to sell loose-leaf encyclopedias. Their relationship finally deteriorates. Mona becomes infatuated with a young, unstable artist, Anastasia (modeled on Jean Kronski, who would commit suicide a few years later). This ménage à trois, which was forecast in the enigmatic final chapter of *Sexus*, humiliates Henry. He is wildly jealous from the beginning, and not without reason. Anastasia is a formidable rival, potentially an insurmountable foe. *Plexus* concludes with a glimpse of Miller's continuing humiliation and failure; but there is now the suggestion that these sufferings will eventually be redeemed by art—by an autobiographical art. Miller likens his early struggles to a "rosy crucifixion." He insists his sufferings are a self-crucifixion. He has martyred himself to the repressive moral constraints of his society in *Sexus* and to the inhuman economic order in *Plexus*. He now anticipates an even more crushing crucifixion in the final volume, *Nexus*.

Miller did not begin writing the final volume of *The Rosy Crucifixion* in earnest until the late fifties. He found it difficult to resume, calling the writing "pick and shovel work."[4] Nevertheless, the transition between *Plexus* and *Nexus* is nearly seamless. *Nexus* is the final station in Miller's "happy" crucifixion. It records the loss of the love that once liberated him but now imprisons and tortures him. Love and its loss are therefore the central themes of *Nexus*, where all relationships are expressed in romantic terms.

In *The Rosy Crucifixion*, Miller creates the myth of his birth as an artist in America. This self-created myth requires its hero to reject the sexual and economic forces that imprison him; it also requires that he reject the one who has freed him, the one he loves more than himself and more than his art. This final loss, which frees Miller to create himself anew in his writing, is a transcendent event. "It is only then, moreover, that the true significance of human suffering becomes clear," he declares. "At the last desperate moment—when one can suffer no more!—something happens which is in the nature of a miracle" (*Plexus*, p. 640). The self-inflicted wounds are healed, the self is freed from all outside powers, and the artist begins to reshape his experiences and discover their essential meanings.

As Mona increases her devotion to another suffering artist, Anastasia, Henry is reduced to a helpless, bitter, manic-depressive animal. He loses his ability to love, to hope, to find joy in living. Defeated, he accepts a job once again—as a gravedigger for Queens County Park Commission—and at this, the lowest point in Miller's travails, Mona and Anastasia abandon him, sailing for Paris together. Miller eventually saves himself by converting his despair into a twenty-six-page outline of his four years with Mona—the outline of the very book he is now writing. It is a Doomsday Book, he declares—"like writing my own epitaph."[5] It is the epitaph of the old self. The new self has another vision, beginning with a disturbing realization:

It was this—our love is ended. That could be the only meaning for planning such a work. I refused, however, to accept this conclusion. I told myself that my true purpose was merely to relate—"merely!"—the story of my misfortunes. But is it possible to write of one's sufferings while one is still suffering? Abélard had done it, to be sure. A sentimental thought now intruded. I would write the book for her—to her—and reading it she would understand, her eyes would be opened, she would help me bury the past, we would begin a new life, a life together . . . true togetherness.

How naive! (*Nexus*, p. 166)

The Rosy Crucifixion is a memorial to the one who was loved, but love itself is in ruins. For the Romantic artist, the end of love is the beginning of art. The death of the muse, of Mona/June, inspires Miller to move from the sufferings of life to the joyous but deathly outlines of

personal art. *Nexus* ends on a happier note: hero and
heroine, reunited, set out for another shore. The essential meaning, however, is darker. The sexual and economic themes of *Sexus* and *Plexus* are transformed by
the romantic and aesthetic themes of *Nexus*. Love and
art are revealed to be symbiotic but also antagonistic.
This irresolvable tension underlies Miller's autobiographical art—in fact, makes the creation of such art
possible.

The *Rosy Crucifixion* is by no means an economical
expression of Miller's vision of his birth as an artist—of
the birth of the Romantic artist in a century hostile to autobiographical writers in the transcendental mode. Nor
is this trilogy a finely-crafted literary work. It is not the
singular achievement that *Tropic of Cancer* is. Nevertheless, it is the most vivid account we have of ordinary,
daily life in the New York of the twenties. Miller captures this life as it was actually lived, no mean achievement. The procession of marginal characters is often
amusing, the frenetic rhythms of their lives powerfully
rendered. The loose structure of *The Rosy Crucifixion* is
often a surprisingly effective solution to a central problem of autobiographical narration, namely the presenta-
tion of actual events without resorting to obvious or ob-
trusive literary devices. The failures of *The Rosy
Crucifixion*—its repetitiveness, its lack of dramatic tension, its frequently uninspired prose—can even bring
the narrative *nearer* to life (although, admittedly, not always *to* life). Those readers and critics who expected *The
Rosy Crucifixion* to do for New York in the twenties
what *Tropic of Cancer* did for Paris in the thirties were
disappointed. Milller was deliberately following the dic-
tates of a new approach to self-narration—discovering,
in fact, a new aesthetic.

He warned Lawrence Durrell the *The Rosy Crucifixion* would surprise, even alarm him:

Lastly, you may not like *R.C.* at all. In some ways it is a reversion to pre-*Tropic* writing. Much more conversation, direct and indirect. Many episodes, dreams, fantasies, throwbacks of all sorts. But a steady forward progression, chronologically, because I am following my notes (written in 1927!).[6]

Durrell was indeed surprised and profoundly disappointed. He immediately expressed what hostile critics ever since have voiced:

I must confess I'm bitterly disappointed in it, despite the fact that it contains some of your very best writing to date. But my dear Henry, the moral vulgarity of so much of it is *artistically* painful. These silly, meaningless scenes which have no raison d'être, no humour, just childish explosions of obscenity—what a pity, what a terrible pity for a major artist not to have critical sense enough to husband his forces, to keep his talent aimed at the target. . . . All the wild resonance of *Cancer* and *Black Spring* has gone, and you have failed to develop what is really new in your prose, and what should set a crown on your work. The new mystical outlines are all there; but they are lost, lost, damn it, in this shower of lavatory filth which no longer seems tonic and bracing, but just excrementitious and sad.[7]

Miller replied that whereas he couldn't judge his own work, he felt he had succeeded, no matter what anyone else thought. He then outlined his defense, forwarding the principles of a new autobiographical aesthetic:

I am writing exactly what I want to write and the way I want to do it. Perhaps it's twaddle, perhaps not. The fact that I put in everything under the sun may be, as you think, because I have lost all sense of values. Again, it may not. I am trying to reproduce in words a block of my life which to me has the utmost significance—every bit of it. . . . I made a herculean effort to represent myself for what I then was. The only artistry I endeavored to employ was the capturing of that other self, those other days. I've been as sincere as I possibly could, maybe too sincere, because it certainly is not a lovely picture I made of myself.[8]

It is as an accurate, *complete* self-portrait that *The Rosy Crucifixion* does succeed. The aesthetic requirements applied to fiction—many of which Miller applied brilliantly to his autobiographical narratives in Paris—are deliberately jettisoned. Miller clearly regards such conventions and techniques as distorting or destructive of the essential truths of self-creation that he is attempting to express. He has become the champion of an antiliterature, or at least of a literature that comes as close to life as possible. Self-creation, he concludes, must be as artless as possible. The book cannot be a fiction: the book must be the self.

This is an extreme aesthetic position and *The Rosy Crucifixion* is an extreme work. Miller would find few critics to defend his trilogy on literary grounds and almost none who understood his aesthetic argument. Nevertheless, he remained satisfied with his achievement and convinced that his approach was correct, that he had finally presented the truths of his own experience openly, directly, and honestly—particularly the truths of his early experience in New York, the decisive period in which he became an autobiographical artist. In a final explanation addressed to Lawrence Durrell, Miller emphasizes again his intentions to write the truth without any proscriptions, even those provided by art:

I have a feeling of regret that I am coming to the end of this priceless material. My autobiographical life will then be done for. What's to follow God alone knows. Maybe I shall retire —defeated. But Larry, I can never go back on what I've written. If it was not good, it was true; if it was not artistic, it was sincere; if it was in bad taste, it was on the side of life. . . . But I had only this one life to record. That passion you sense to be lacking has been put into the minus side . . . . Perhaps in the summing up, my life will be seen to be a huge pyramid erected over a minus sign. Still, nevertheless, a pyramid. Perhaps better understood when placed upside down.[9]

8

𝅥𝅥𝅥

Big Sur:
Paradise and Beyond

For Henry Miller, Big Sur was Eden in the New World, a place as primitive, spectacular, untrammeled, and visionary as the Old World Eden he had discovered in Greece. During the first year he lived at Big Sur (1944), Miller cultivated the austere life of a Tibetan monk, until remarrying in December. With his new wife, Janina Martha Lepska, and eventually their two children, Val and Tony, Henry was content at first. The rural life was fatiguing and there was little enough hard cash flowing in from Miller's writing, but he enjoyed his rugged paradise, so distant in every way from New York or Paris. The poisoned fruit in this idyllic garden was the marriage itself. Henry and Lepska were of conflicting temperaments. They clashed frequently, especially over matters of child rearing. By 1951 they had separated for good.

It was at this low point in paradise that Miller began to write *The Books in My Life*, a long account of what he had read and how it had influenced him. The idea for this project was implanted by Lawrence Clark Powell, a UCLA librarian who had already persuaded Miller to deposit his letters, manuscripts, and assorted records in a special "Henry Miller Archives" on the campus. Coincidentally, Powell had been a student at the Lycée Carnot the same year (1932) Miller taught there, although they did not meet then. Books had always been an essential part of Miller's life, as real as any actual event or acquaintance. *The Books in My Life* became another kind of personal narrative, Miller said, "to supplement the autobiographical 'novels' I have written—round out the picture of my life, so to speak."[1] In the preface to this book about books—which was more a book about Henry Miller, of course—he termed the composition a "self-examination" and announced he would deal "with books as vital experience."[2]

The Books in My Life is chiefly of interest for certain passages that reveal new information or elucidate crucial literary themes. We learn, for example, that Miller has not read all the great autobiographers (not Rousseau, not De Quincey, not even Henry Adams), but that he has a special understanding of the role of children's books in forming the imaginative dispositions of authors and readers. We discover how Miller defines romance literature and the dark, incestuous forces it embodies (pp. 93–97); how Miller views his affinity with Walt Whitman (pp. 104, 221–243); and how he sees himself as an American:

I feel least of all like an American, though I am probably more an American than anything else. The American in me which I acknowledge and recognize, the American which I salute, if I must put it that way, is the aboriginal being, the seed and the promise, which took shape in "the common man" dedicating his soul to a new experiment, establishing on virgin soil "the city of brotherly love." (p. 253)

These and other discussions in *The Books in My Life* make it clear that the mysticism and metaphysics Miller mixes in his narratives (ever more thickly after Paris) are derived from American transcendentalism—from Whitman, Emerson, and Thoreau—rather than from the Eastern traditions of Lao-tze and Krishnamurti.

While *The Books in My Life* contains remarkable passages, it is overdrawn and windy. It lacks the coherence of Miller's finest work in the fifties, *Big Sur and the Oranges of Hieronymus Bosch* (1957). This account of

the early years of Miller's life at Big Sur parallels Thoreau's account of his life at Walden. Miller's twentieth-
century Walden is a natural paradise where the self can
assume its genuine Adamic dimensions and judge the
rest of the nation from a transcendent, rural perspective.

In *Big Sur and the Oranges of Hieronymus Bosch,*
Miller writes three evocative prefaces: the first concerns
personal history ("Chronological"); the second, Big Sur's
pure, natural form ("Topographical"); and the third, a
New World myth of time and timelessness ("In the Beginning"). Outlining his personal history, Miller concentrates on his arrival in California and the four places he
has lived at Big Sur—the last being a house on
Partington Ridge where Miller resided from 1947 until
the sixties. The entire chronology, written in simple, direct, unadorned prose, is hardly more than a page.
Twice that space is then devoted to a portrait of the
place, which for Miller becomes "an initiation into a new
way of life."[3] He recounts the civilized and geological
history of Big Sur, noting, "It is a region where extremes
meet, a region where one is always conscious of weather,
of space, of grandeur, and of eloquent silence" (p. 4). It
is the stark wilderness, one of the final stretches of the
frontier that, as fact and image, has shaped the American
experience from the beginning. In a final preface, we see
that what fascinates Miller is the primitive element, the
inhuman image of eternal nature: "At dawn its majesty is
almost painful to behold. That same prehistoric look.
The look of always. Nature smiling at herself in the mirror of eternity" (p. 8). It is the world at the Creation, the
world that Whitman created in his earthy, transcendental poetry, that Thoreau found at Walden, that Miller
creates in his own image at Big Sur.

After these evocations, which link personal and social history to nature and the infinite, Miller elaborates
on his central theme: namely, that Big Sur is a paradise
where the individual can create a new self. Miller cele-

brates a generation of modern Thoreaus returning to the wilderness:

> Utterly disillusioned, this new breed of experimenter is reso-
> lutely turning his back on all that he once held true and viable,
> and is making a valiant effort to start anew. Starting anew, for
> this type, means leading a vagrant's life, tackling anything,
> clinging to nothing, reducing one's needs and one's desires,
> and eventually—out of a wisdom born of desperation—lead-
> ing the life of an artist. Not, however, the type of artist we
> are familiar with. An artist, rather, whose sole interest is in
> creating, an artist who is indifferent to reward, fame, success.
> (p. 17)

Often Miller echoes the hortatory pronouncements that Thoreau broadcast to his urban neighbors from Walden a century earlier, as in this call to his neighbors to awaken from their lives of "quiet desperation":

> How illustrative, this attitude, of the woeful resignation
> men and women succumb to! Surely every one realizes, at
> some point along the way, that he is capable of living a far bet-
> ter life than the one he has chosen. What stays him, usually, is
> the fear of sacrifices involved. (Even to relinquish his chains
> seems like a sacrifice.) Yet everyone knows that nothing is ac-
> complished without sacrifice.
> The longing for paradise, whether here on earth or in the
> beyond, has almost ceased to be. Instead of an *idée-force* it has
> become an *idée fixe*. From a potent myth it has degenerated
> into a taboo. Men will sacrifice their lives to bring about a bet-
> ter world—whatever that may mean—but they will not budge
> an inch to attain paradise. (p. 24)

Yet it is in this natural paradise that the solitary self can apprehend the unity of the world:

> Only when we are truly alone does the fullness and richness of
> life reveal itself to us. In simplifying our lives, everything ac-
> quires a significance hitherto unknown. When we are one with
> ourselves the most insignificant blade of grass assumes its
> proper place in the universe. (p. 34)

The oranges of Hieronymus Bosch in his triptych, "The Millenium," enter the title of *Big Sur* to emphasize the hallucinatory, transcendent reality of the place, with its echoes "of an age when man was one with all creation" (p. 23). Bosch's painted oranges are oranges of a super-reality, just as Big Sur is the image of the expanded soul:

The oranges of Bosch's "Millenium," as I said before, exhale this dreamlike reality which constantly eludes us and which is the very substance of life. They are far more delectable, far more potent, than the Sunkist oranges we daily consume in the naive belief that they are laden with wonder-working vitamins. The millenial oranges which Bosch created restore the soul; the ambiance in which he suspended them is the everlasting one of spirit become real. (pp. 28–29)

What keeps Miller's usual rhetoric of transcendentalism from becoming insufferable in *Big Sur and the Oranges of Hieronymus Bosch* is an abundance of concrete detail and practical observation. The place is, as Miller notes, "so spectacular, so complete in itself," that one is at first overwhelmed (p. 36). Soon, however, one adjusts to paradise, becomes bored, and begins to be quarrelsome, even unhappy. "The one difference between Big Sur and other 'ideal' spots is that here you get it quick and get it hard," Miller cautions. "The result is that you either come to grips with yourself or else turn tail and seek some other spot in which to nourish your illusions" (p. 37). The requirements of this natural paradise are harsh but rewarding:

When all is said and done, there remains the inescapable fact that to keep a footing here taxes all one's resources. One may be capable, practical, determined, persevering, full of vitality, yet never quite equal to the challenge which is constantly imposed. It is all thrown at you pell-mell: landscapes, seascapes, forests, streams, birds of passage, weeds, pests, rattlesnakes, gophers, earwigs, misfits, vagabonds, sunsets, rainbows, yarrow, hollyhocks, and that leech of the plant world called the morning-glory. Even the rocks are seductive and hypnotic.

And where else on this earth will you find a towering wall of fog advancing from the date line with a knife-blue crest behind which a setting sun shoots out "squirrels and lightning"? (p. 36)

The heart of the book, the fifteen chapters of the section titled "Peace and Solitude: a Potpourri," is an elaboration of the real and the metaphysical at Big Sur. In introducing this potpourri, Miller warns that he will tell his story in "disorderly fashion" and that "cause and event, chronology, order of any kind—except the illogical order of life itself—is absent" (p. 42). Actually *Big Sur and the Oranges of Hieronymus Bosch* has an exceptionally well-structured thematic order. The anecdotes and portraits are not aimlessly arranged; they are related to Miller's vision of natural paradise, and each tells of man's ability to live in accordance with natural law. Miller begins by dismissing the sensationalists who come to Big Sur expecting to find a "new cult of sex and anarchy" presided over by an author of banned books.[4] Miller has in fact fashioned a new image of himself, one that eschews gross sensuality and sexual freedom and emphasizes self-discipline and higher knowledge. The residents at Big Sur whom Miller portrays are uncompromising artists and rebels who have withdrawn to find a new, simpler life in the country.

Part of the self-image Miller creates at Big Sur is that of the delighted father of two small children. He encourages their energy and anarchy, and clashes with their mother, Lepska, over principles of parenting. Once, Miller's own remembered childhood figured prominently in his writing; now, it is the childhood of his own children about which he writes. The child-rearing philosophy Miller champions, of course, is Romantic and antidisciplinary. Viewing a strict education as destructive of innocent vision and parental authority as cruelty, Miller favors a "natural" approach to parenting. When put to the test as a single parent (after Lepska leaves Big Sur in 1951), Miller tries valiantly to be the perfect mother and father. Eventually he must admit his defeat. It is not until he brings his fourth wife, Eve McClure, to Big Sur in 1952 that he can again live with his children.

Like Thoreau, Miller divides his account of natural paradise into related thematic units. Miller's chief concerns are nature, art, economy, and self-knowledge— themes familiar to any reader of Emerson or Thoreau. Invariably these themes arise from the daily circumstances of Big Sur. One morning in 1944, for example, Miller receives a long letter from Maurice Girodias, son of Jack Kahane and now owner of Obelisk Press in Paris, informing Miller that he is due some forty thousand dollars in royalties. For the first time in his life, Miller is rich, but he is no longer so entranced by the world's definition of riches. It is just as well. Miller cannot receive his royalties so long as he lives in America; post-World War II currency and export laws forbid it. Miller's only alternative is to return to France and enjoy his fortune there. He dallies and eventually stays at Big Sur. (In fact, his mother was ill in New York City and Henry refused to abandon her. He also did not want to take his newborn daughter, Valentine, to live in France, where medical services and other conditions were in a shambles.) Above all, Miller will not be tempted away from his paradise at any price. His wages are now those of another world:

And only yesterday—what a coincidence!—coming from a walk in the hills, a thin, transparent fog touching everything with quick-silver fingers, only yesterday, I say, coming in view of our grounds, I suddenly recognized it to be "the wild park" which I had described myself to be in this same *Capricorn*. There it was, swimming in an underwater light, the trees spaced just right, the willow in front bowing to the willow in back, the roses in full bloom, the pampas grass just beginning to don its plumes of gold, the hollyhocks standing out like starved sentinels with big, bright buttons, the birds darting from tree to tree, calling to one another imperiously, and Eve standing barefoot in her Garden of Eden with a grub hoe in her hand, while Dante Alighieri, pale as alabaster and with only his head showing above the rim, was making to slake his awesome thirst in the bird bath under the elm. (pp. 129–130)

Among the Waldenesque lessons Miller learns at Big Sur are self-reliance and cosmic nonresistance. He rejects convention and conventional wisdom, simplifies his life, and trains his satirical sights on a nation that rejects the higher idealism manifest in nature.

Miller did most of his writing on *Big Sur and the Oranges of Hieronymus Bosch* in 1955, incorporating in the published version a related piece he had composed earlier, "Paradise Lost." This piece recounts the disastrous visit of Conrad Moricand, destitute dandy and French astrologer, to Big Sur.[5] The Moricand portrait is, in the opinion of Miller's biographer, Jay Martin, "one of the best works composed during this period." Martin adds:

The encounter with Moricand generated the kind of misery in Henry that he had experienced in 1930 and 1931 in Paris. And hopeless misery was, for him, the first spark of the creative fires.[6]

The "Paradise Lost" section is indeed as commanding and effortless in appearance as Miller's earlier short narratives. Miller had been acquainted with Moricand for several years in Paris, but they were never the closest of friends. Nevertheless Miller, who now was having difficulties in his relationship with Lepska and had very little money to spare, responded with extreme generosity when Moricand wrote begging to be taken in. In March 1947 Miller cabled Moricand: "Our home is yours." Moricand accepted the offer at once. Miller signed papers making himself financially responsible for Moricand in America and sent a ticket for the trip from Paris to Los Angeles. (This alone cost Miller six months' earnings.) Moricand arrived in February 1948. Lepska was pregnant with a second child, but she proved tolerant of this "lifetime" guest. Henry gave up his cheery office space to Moricand; Moricand, however, was anything but comfortable. The cabin depressed him, the rural isolation terrified him. Moricand was an urban being, cosmopolitan and hypersensitive. His personality was one that invited and cultivated gloom. The winter rains crushed whatever optimism he might have summoned, and by the end of March, Moricand insisted on leaving. At Miller's expense he stayed first in Monterey, where his skin rash was treated, then for an extended period in a San Francisco hotel. As all his friends had so confidently predicted, Miller's generosity now turned into an interminable nightmare.

Miller's narrative of this "devil in paradise" at Big Sur is little more than a statement of the facts. It seldom focuses on Miller himself, except when drawing a self-portrait by contrast:

My native optimism and recklessness complemented his ingrained pessimism and cautiousness. I was frank and outspoken, he judicious and reserved. My tendency was to exfoliate in all directions; he, on the other hand, had narrowed his interests and focused on them with his whole being. He had all the reason and logic of the French, whereas I often contradicted myself and flew off at tangents. (p. 277)

Miller is the happy man of action—the American —while Moricand is the man restricted by the lines in his astrological chart—"a victim doomed to live a dolorous, circumscribed life"—in other words, the European (p. 285). In an argument over determinism and free will, Miller makes this international conflict plain, telling Moricand:

I am still very much of an American. That is to say, naive, optimistic, gullible. Perhaps all I gained from the fruitful years I spent in France was a strengthening and deepening of my own inner spirit. In the eyes of a European, what am I but an American to the core, an American who exposes his Americanism like a sore. Like it or not, I am a believer in miracles. Any deprivation I suffered was my own doing. (p. 319)

While the appearance of Moricand elicits a marvelous evocation of Miller's Paris days, it threatens the heart of paradise. Moricand acts like a "spoiled child," a "leech," an insufferable egotist:

Suddenly it seemed as if the ground opened under my feet. Here he was, safe and secure, with a haven for the rest of his life in the midst of *"un vrai paradis,"* and he must have Yardley's talcum powder! Then and there I should have obeyed my instinct and said, "Beat it! Get back to your Purgatory!" (p. 301)

The devil, of course, is not so easily expelled from Paradise. For more than a year Moricand hangs on at Miller's expense in America. Miller eventually tells us in his best matter-of-fact style that Moricand has returned to France and applied for admission to a Swiss home for the aged on the Avenue de St. Mandé in Paris:

It was an institution founded by his own parents. Here he chose a small cell giving on the courtyard, where from his window he could see the placque commemorating the inauguration of the establishment by his mother and his brother, Dr. Ivan Moricand. (p. 385)

Moricand dies suddenly there, we are told, at 10:30 P.M., August 31, 1954.

Perhaps to transform this sad note, Miller adds an epilogue to *Big Sur*. Its subject is letter writing; its theme, the vital relation of art to Miller's life:

The only life! Why in hell was I born a writer? Maybe I'm not a writer any more. But deep down I know that, after I have had my fling, I will go back to the typewriter. I will die sitting at the typewriter, in all probability. I know it. But now and then I allow myself the luxury of thinking that one day I will chuck it all. I will do nothing. *Just live.* (p. 393)

This is a fine epitaph for Miller's literary career. He could not stop writing in Paris, in Greece, even in the earthly paradise of Big Sur. It was as much a part of his life as life itself, as the potpourri of living forms and millennial oranges that brought him a measure of peace and solitude:

And that is why I choose to remain here, on the slopes of the Santa Lucia, where to give thanks to the Creator comes natural and easy. Out yonder they may curse, revile and torture one another, defile all the human instincts, make a shambles of creation (if it were in their power), but here, no, here it is unthinkable, here there is abiding peace, the peace of God, and the serene security created by a handful of good neighbors living at one with the creature world, with noble, ancient trees, scrub and sagebrush, wild lilac and lovely lupin, with poppies and buzzards, eagles and humming birds, gophers and rattlesnakes, and sea and sky unending. (p. 404)

Although not as profound or revolutionary a work as *Tropic of Cancer* or even *The Colossus of Maroussi*, *Big Sur and the Oranges of Hieronymus Bosch* elicited considerable praise from the critics. The portrait of Conrad Moricand was especially admired. In England, Sir Herbert Read wrote that it "has the vividness of seventeenth-century Aubrey and the psychological penetration of twentieth-century Proust."[7] In America, Phoebe Adams hailed it as "a small masterpiece" and added: "It is appallingly alive, tightly organized, penetrating, and it never wavers from that colloquial, conversational prose that is one of Mr. Miller's finest achievements."[8]

Miller's years at Big Sur, despite the streams of visitors, were as peaceful and solitudinous as any he would ever know. By the time his Paris works were legally published in America, beginning in 1961, this coastal paradise would be past regaining and privacy an impossibility. The fifties was a quiet decade for Miller; the sixties and seventies were loud, chaotic, distracting. *Big Sur and the Oranges of Hieronymus Bosch* would be Miller's last extended personal narrative. In the remaining twenty-four years of his life, however, he would not cease writing. He would produce numerous essays, some with original power and insight. Sheer longevity allowed Miller another kind of triumph: he would outlive the censors who had locked his masterpieces overseas in the vaults of France. The revolution in moral and literary tastes he had dreamed of would soon come to pass.

The fifties was a generally serene prelude to that chaotic decade of fortune and fame, the sixties. Big Sur still contained intimations of paradise. Miller enjoyed his two young children; Eve proved a less quarrelsome mate than Lepska. It was also at Big Sur that he was reunited with old acquaintances. In 1953 George Katsimbalis visited. He was the great Greek monologist, the model for Miller's colossus of Maroussi. In November of the same year Miller was reunited with Alfred Perlès, his oldest and best friend of the Paris years. Perlès was writing a memoir, and Miller now assisted in shaping the not-altogether reliable but always amusing *My Friend Henry Miller*.[9] The next year (in June 1954) Miller was visited by his first daughter, Barbara, whom he had not seen since the "rosy crucifixion" days, the late twenties in Brooklyn. Henry found this reconciliation with "the child of his youth" (Barbara was now thirty-four years old) particularly satisfying. Far more traumatic, however, was his reunion with his mother on her deathbed in 1956. Henry left Big Sur and lived in New York for four months to be at her side. Whereas he dismissed her death as unimportant and final, Miller had by no means come to terms with this relationship. More than twenty years later, in *Mother, China, and the World Beyond* (1977) Miller imagines a reconciliation with his mother, whom, he declares, "I hated all my life," but from whom he still seeks the love that never existed.[10] The story is cast in the form of a dream of the afterlife. Having died, Miller is immediately greeted by his mother. She is radiant for the first time. She is wise and loving. It is in this dreamworld—a pleasant limbo between earth and eternity—that there is finally genuine compassion and understanding on both sides. They only meet in passing, however; Henry is heading out to find "another Heaven," while his mother is returning to earth to begin another round of suffering. As they part, Henry shouts his love and his mother faintly smiles. "I was alone, but more alone than I had ever felt on Earth," Miller remarks as the dream ends and the finality of separation and solitude begins. "And I would be alone, perhaps, for centuries or, who knows, perhaps through all eternity."[11]

Three more significant reunions occurred at the beginning of Miller's eighth decade. In September 1961 Henry agreed to meet with June in New York. Time had not been kind to June. She had married Stratford Corbett, an Air Force officer, after her divorce from Miller in the thirties, but she had been on her own since 1942. Several times she had begged Miller for financial assistance during the Big Sur years, and he had responded as best he could. Meeting her face to face after twenty-eight years, Miller was overcome with anguish. June, not yet sixty, appeared to be on her deathbed, a zombie, her zest for life and her strength utterly depleted.[12] Henry could do little for her. She seemed an empty shell.

The next year Henry was reunited with Anaïs Nin. They had not seen each other in sixteen years. Now they agreed upon a project that would become Miller's *Letters to Anaïs Nin* (1965), a collection of some of his best letters. (It also marked the first time Anaïs agreed to make her personal relationship with Henry public.) Earlier, while a judge at the International Film Festival in

Cannes (1960), Miller was also reunited with Lawrence Durrell. Later their correspondence would prove as dramatic as a novel.[13] (Both Miller and Durrell were masters of letter writing; they had composed several epistolary duets over the years.) While Miller would never again produce works as original as those he had written in Paris or as monumental as those from Big Sur, he could now call upon an immense accumulation of previously unpublished letters written during those periods to keep his name before readers and critics.

Much of Miller's literary capital seemed untouchable; the censors were as vigilant as ever. For several years, nevertheless, Barney Rosset of Grove Press had been badgering Miller to sign a contract that would allow him to publish the Paris works in America—thereby challenging the censorship laws. Miller hesitated; he was content with his underground reputation and the modest income his books generated even when banned. He was apprehensive about the burdens he would have to shoulder if he became a cause célèbre in his own country. At one point in their negotiations, Miller wrote Rosset: "As for a sudden increase in fortune, it would undoubtedly cause me more harm than good." Miller's intention in his banned autobiographies, he maintained, had been to awaken his readers to a transcendent reality and to inspire revolt, "not merely to titillate and amuse." He told Rosset he feared he would be known only as "the King of Smut."[14]

All that Miller feared did come to pass when Rosset published *Tropic of Cancer* on June 24, 1961, in America, twenty-seven years after its appearance in France. The first week sixty-eight thousand copies were sold; by year's end the sales totaled a hundred thousand in hardback and over one million in softback. Miller kept out of public view. He moved into a furnished room in the Pacific Palisades area of Los Angeles to be near his two children, who were living with their mother, Lepska. Despite the fortune his unbanned books were now making, he had little money. Alimony and child support took some of his earnings; taxes and repaid loans took the greater share. By 1964 Miller had given away over a hundred thousand dollars to friends he owed or who were in need—a late but quite generous repayment for all the loans he had procured over the last half century.[15] Despite these and other financial problems, however, Miller would be reasonably secure and comfortable for the rest of his life. In February 1963 he purchased a large, respectable house on Ocampo Drive in Pacific Palisades where he would live with his family until his death.

The publication of *Tropic of Cancer* in America brought about the end of literary censorship, at least on the grounds of obscenity. Grove Press fought a number of *Tropic of Cancer* skirmishes in municipal and state courts across the nation (sixty such cases in the first year alone). Almost two hundred of America's most prominent authors signed a statement supporting Miller and condemning literary censorship. By the time the U.S. Supreme Court lifted the ban on publication of *Tropic of Cancer* (1964), Henry Miller was the most litigated author of all time. The legal confrontations initiated by the works of James Joyce and D. H. Lawrence had concluded with Henry Miller. The *Tropic of Cancer* cases soon found their way into academic studies of censorship.[16]

The Rosy Crucifixion was, of course, far more sexually graphic than Miller's other works, but by the time it was published in America (1965), the public was reconciled to the wider principle *Tropic of Cancer* had established. Sexual content alone no longer disqualified the publication of a serious literary work. (Ironically, it was in France that this principle was now ignored. In March 1964 Maurice Girodias was fined, sentenced to one year in prison, and forbidden to publish anything in France for twenty years because he had published one "obscene" book, namely Miller's *Sexus*.) The climate had been transformed from one extreme to the other in America. *Sexus*, *Plexus*, and *Nexus* suddenly caused only the slightest stir. Jay Martin remarks:

Once these books might have created a storm of controversy, but now there was no great opposition. Americans seemed to feel that "the Miller case," the fight against censorship, had been settled over *Tropic of Cancer*. Very few persons live to see the triumph of a great cultural revolution for which they are mainly responsible. But Miller did live to see a total reversal in American laws and social mores concerning the circulation of explicitly sexual writing, largely as a result of his own books. As H.L. Mencken had predicted thirty years earlier, his triumph came quickly, like a landslide, when at last it came. [17]

In the last two decades of his life, the sixties and seventies, Henry Miller wrote in two main veins. First he recounted again and again the earlier events of his life, particularly of the Paris period. He did not seem to tire of repeating the "legend of himself" that had already achieved its definitive versions years earlier in *Tropic of Cancer*, *Tropic of Capricorn*, *Black Spring*, *The Rosy Crucifixion*, and other narratives. One of the better examples of this retelling of the already told was *My Life and Times* (1971), a coffee table book produced by Playboy Press. [18] The photographs, the reproductions of paintings, the pages from notebooks, letters, and manuscripts are interesting, but Miller's text—a casual memoir—simply recapitulates the events in the autobiographies. Much the same can be said for the many published and recorded interviews—some quite lengthy—that Miller granted in his later years. [19] The most important new information about Miller's past, his actual relationships with other writers, and his thoughts on a range of current matters, including literary theories and

the genesis of his own work, can be gleaned from his collected letters, edited by others (although the editing of
his correspondence was always closely monitored by
Miller himself).[20]

The other category of Miller's later writings includes a number of chapbooks—original compositions,
sometimes addressing current matters rather than those
of the past. One of the best of these personal essays is *Insomnia; Or, the Devil at Large* (1971), a lively but sad account of Miller's fifth and final marriage.[21] In 1966 he
met Japanese jazz singer Hiroko Tokuda, and after a
courtship (like one an elderly admirer might have staged
when infatuated with June in the twenties) Henry and
Hoki were married on September 10, 1967. Miller was
then seventy-seven years old; his bride was nearly fifty
years younger. Hoki moved out before Miller turned
eighty (a birthday he commemorated with some melan-
choly in yet another chapbook essay).[22]

Despite failing health (that severely affected his mo-
bility and eyesight), Miller did not abandon writing. He
projected a multivolume "book of friends" in 1972, and
the first entry, a collection of vigorous memoirs of his
earliest Brooklyn acquaintances, appeared in 1976.[23] It
shed new light on the actual personages who had served
as models for some of the major characters in *Black
Spring, Tropic of Capricorn*, and especially *The Rosy
Crucifixion*. The second volume (*My Bike and Other
Friends*) appeared in 1978 and was a collection of portraits of the friends he had included in *Big Sur and the
Oranges of Hieronymus Bosch*.[24] He completed this
second volume in spite of the illness and paralysis that
confined him virtually without respite to his home. Miller was approaching his eighty-sixth birthday when he
completed the third volume (*Joey*) in 1979.[25] *Joey* is
perhaps the most remarkable part of his trilogy—a vi-
brant portrait of Alfred Perlès, a final meditation on
Anaïs Nin (who, like so many of Miller's younger ac-

quaintances, had preceded him in death), and thirteen
new essays on "other women" in his life, from the mistress he had taken at eighteen to his latest companion,
Brenda Venus, with whom he posed in a 1979 picture on
the back cover. In his preface to this final gallery of acquaintances, Miller writes, "I had thought that I would
do very little further writing, if any at all," but the desire
to define himself once again, as well as capture "the essence and the fragrance" of the past, was irresistible.[26]
In the closing lines, celebrating his latest love, Brenda
Venus, Miller is still able to summon his sense of wonder
and adventure:

Where will this strange creature lead me, I wonder? To what
strange shores? I have put myself in her hands. Lead me, O
blessed one, wherever![27]

These were to be the final lines of Miller's final book.

Another book did appear the next year—*The
World of Lawrence* (1980)—but it was a selection from
Miller's unpublished study of D. H. Lawrence that pre-
dated the publication of his first book, *Tropic of Cancer*.[28] Appearing in the year of his death, it reminded
readers of how brilliant, if unruly, Miller had been in his
beginnings in Paris. He was not able then to organize his
sprawling materials, but he was on the track he would
follow. His criticism of D. H. Lawrence in 1932 was a
mode of self-expression; and his definition of the Romantic artist in the twentieth century—of the artist Miller
would become—had taken its vital form:

Strange as it may seem today to say, the aim of life is to live,
and to live means to be aware, joyously, drunkenly, serenely,
divinely *aware*. In this state of god-like awareness one sings; in
this realm the world exists as poem. No why or wherefore, no
direction, no goal, no striving, no evolving. Like the enigmatic
Chinese, one is rapt by the ever-changing spectacle of passing
phenomena. This is the sublime, the amoral state of the artist,
he who lives only in the moment, the visionary moment of ut-

ter, far-seeing lucidity. Such clear, icy sanity that it seems like madness. By the force and power of the artist's vision the static, synthetic whole which is called the world is destroyed. The artist gives back to us a vital, singing universe, alive in all its parts.[29]

In the opening lines of *The World of Lawrence*, Miller wrote, "As everyone knows, the body of Lawrence's work forms a huge self-portrait."[30] This remark applies even more forcibly to Miller's immense but then unwritten canon. Perhaps what is most striking throughout this book is the consistency of Miller's vision, its coherence through decades of success and failure, of unpredictable and sometimes monstrous change. Although written before *Tropic of Cancer* erupted on the map of world literature, this passage gives us a remarkable summary of Miller's literary career fifty years before it would end. He is really speaking of himself here:

In his individual works—and this is more particularly true of the Dionysian type—the artist seems fragmented. But each individual work is a complete representation of his momentary wholeness. He lives and dies in each work. His works are a succession of births and deaths, a spiritual progression, a quickening that mocks the slow, torpid life-death, or death-life, of the mass about. Through his inexhaustible roles he records the changeless ego, through the poem the eternal *how* of things. He is like the *ouroboros*, the snake that swallows its own tail. He consumes himself, and in devouring himself he completes the picture of the world. He is the circle without beginning or end.[31]

So begins and ends Miller's own fifty-year circle. His *World of Lawrence*, coinciding with the fiftieth anniversary of D. H. Lawrence's death, also commemorates the year of Miller's death.

Miller's was an ordinary death, befitting this self-described "Brooklyn boy." He died in his sleep on June 7, 1980, in the fiercely respectable two-story house in Pacific Palisades, the dwelling so at odds with the world's image of the ultimate literary desperado. Obituaries praising Miller the artist appeared around the world. One of the briefest but most accurate was written by his first and most important publisher in America, James Laughlin:

People who only read the Tropics books, may well have thought of Henry Miller as some sort of a sex fiend or monster. Nothing could be further from the truth. He was, as a person, mild, charming and enormously generous to others. Most of his royalties he gave away to help writers who were in difficult straits. The great quality of his writing was that it was truly American. He worked out an idiom for his expression which was in complete accord with colloquial American speech, and therein lay a great part of its power.[32]

9

Autobiography in America

Henry Miller never lacked a stalwart legion of detractors. His strengths as a writer were counterbalanced by obvious weaknesses. When his command of the colloquial style faltered, he produced some of the most awkward prose of the age. His surrealistic effusions could become utterly confusing; his dadaistic pastiches puerile and self-indulgent. Many reviewers lambasted the Miller philosophy as dime-store mysticism. His vitriolic denouncements of America were judged to be facile or offensive; his celebrations of particular artists, uncritical and self-serving; his metaphysical pronouncements, glib or idiotic. In their closing arguments, those prosecuting Miller for literary charlatanism called attention to his literary decline. If *Tropic of Cancer*, his first book, showed promise—indeed, was a minor classic—was it also not a fluke? Each succeeding work was a step down the ladder of literary excellence. At the bottom rung was *The Rosy Crucifixion*, which took formlessness and self-indulgence beyond the most generously drawn limits.

Such arguments notwithstanding, Henry Miller remains a great American writer. Because his fall from the literary heights was so extended, it is easy to lose sight of the contributions he made to twentieth-century literature. If he outlived the artist he had been, perhaps coming generations will more easily forgive him the sin of longevity. *Tropic of Cancer* is a modern masterpiece.

Black Spring, Tropic of Capricorn, and *The Colossus of Maroussi* are solid, innovative works. Miller was a writer on the side of excess, extravagance, and extremes; he did not appeal to readers and critics who demanded subtlety, irony, and wit, or a spare style and an unflagging control of the medium. He was a comedian, not a tragedian; a Romantic, not an ironist; an autobiographer, not a novelist. His work is uneven, but Miller's entire canon, even to its weakest link, is an unparalleled achievement in personal narration.

A writer's importance is not ultimately a product of his shortcomings. The strengths are what endure, and Miller had exceptional strengths. His greatest achievements were as a surrealist, as a vernacular humorist, as a transcendentalist, and as an autobiographer. In these four respects Miller ranks with the best writers of this century.

Before Henry Miller, it is difficult to speak of a major American surrealist, unless one broadens this category to include Edgar Allan Poe. Miller made surrealism an integral element of narrative prose. He also fashioned his own distinctive surrealistic style. Miller's blend of unconscious association, word play, and savage imagery powerfully expressed the rebellious energy of an individual narrator in a collapsing culture. Surrealism was an appropriate technique to reflect the social theme of disintegration, a technique that later writers from William Burroughs to Norman Mailer would also use. Frequently Miller's surrealism was modulated into dadaistic satire and burlesque; and when sheer playfulness and grotesque imagery merge, Miller's prose is at its best. No writer before or since has rendered so successfully the rhythms of chaos, the beauty of violence, and the high spirits of disorder. Miller's improbable, original juxtapositions also welded the squalid to the sublime, resulting in an original order of beauty. As the surrealist of chaos, Miller found the ideal literary technique to express one truth of the modern experience, the splendor of disintegration:

I have never felt any antagonism for or anxiety over the anarchy represented by the prevailing forms of art; on the contrary, I have always welcomed the dissolving influences. In an age marked by dissolution, liquidation seems to me a virtue, nay a moral imperative. Not only have I never felt the least desire to conserve, bolster up or buttress anything, but I might say that I have always looked upon decay as being just as wonderful and rich an expression of life as growth.[1]

Surrealism was Miller's means to express the dissolution that was a vital part of life; he mastered that technique as no prose writer had.

Less spectacular than Miller's surreal imagery and dadaistic compositions, but more fundamental to his art, is the colloquial style of his narratives. Miller's voice is pure American vernacular—the rough and tumble, loud and laughing (almost belching) voice of the streets. It is the crude, authentic voice of working-class, urban America. Many critics have praised this apparently effortless, "natural" prose style; in fact, Miller toiled ten years to perfect it. By the end of the thirties, George Orwell was arguing that Miller had revitalized English prose. The flowing rhythms of Miller's voice were "quite different from the flat cautious statements and snack-bar dialects" then in fashion, and superior to them.[2]

In the twentieth century, the colloquial voice became *the* voice of American literature. Sherwood Anderson, Gertrude Stein, William Faulkner, Ernest Hemingway, and others refined the colloquial style in prose; the best American poets, with William Carlos Williams the modern source, also turned toward the vigor and rhythms of common native speech.[3] Henry Miller's version of the colloquial, however, grew from the original nineteenth-century vernacular strain, the tradition headed by Mark Twain. Miller's vernacular was largely unrefined and stridently "unliterary." His style was crude, rambling, excessive, suited for exaggeration and bombast, for anecdote and protest. Above all, Miller's vernacular was the vehicle for comedy and satire. In this sense he followed Twain rather than Williams, but he departed from Twain, too. His voice was rougher, his wit grosser, than Twain's. Miller's vernacular humor was faithful to its environs, to the middle and lower strata of industrialized, urban America. It was a humor of hopelessness and outrage, grim but sidesplitting. If the satire was bitter—as in the Cosmodemonic Telegraph Company episodes—it also possessed an element of burlesque. Miller was the least genteel of our major comic writers, and his extended jokes were often sexual. Thus, the grotesque exaggeration of fundamental realities— the realities of the body and the senses —formed the basis of his comedy.

Miller's humor was limited—it lacked irony and wit—but it was direct and powerful. Aiming low, Miller often opened a higher spiritual vista. His crude humor could dissolve all conventions, distinctions, and barriers, exposing the individual to an animalistic, yet curiously divine, essence. Miller could create only one vernacular hero—himself—to place beside the likes of Huck Finn or Hank Morgan; but if he lacked Twain's range and depth in humor, he shared his iconoclastic vision. It is the intent of vernacular humor to show that the morals and mores of society are ridiculous and possibly destructive to individuals. Like Twain, Miller succeeded in this intent. In the process, he created a vernacular hero and voice as distinct and genuine as those of Twain.

As a humorist, Miller writes in the nineteenth-century native vernacular tradition, but without genteel restraints. As a visionary, he draws upon America's most idealistic tradition—that of transcendentalism—and darkens it for a darker time. Miller rejects most American institutions past or present, but as Ihab Hassan points out:

There is no doubt that Miller belongs to a distinct American tradition. Emerson, Thoreau, Whitman—authors Miller idolized—are fathers to this brash child. He venerates, even as he shares with them, their clear concern with spirit, their urgent sense of Being. He takes joy in their anarchy and self-reliance and in their generous capacity for love. He exults in their democratic availability to experience and their prophetic distrust of power.[4]

Miller is America's foremost twentieth-century transcendentalist. He single-handedly revitalized and enlarged upon that tradition, central to our thought and literature, but seemingly out of tune with the nightmare realities of the age.[5] Miller, however, could be Walt Whitman without democratic vistas. He could invert the bright, optimistic idealism of Emerson, yet retain the hope and healthy spirits of Thoreau. At bottom, Miller believed in a transcendent reality, in a metaphysical self that was autonomous and unlimited. The twentieth century seemed antithetical to such self-conceptions and ruthlessly oppressive to full individual freedoms. Yet in Miller's view this did not invalidate the idealism of the transcendentalists; it simply made more urgent than ever the restorative visions of Emerson, Thoreau, and Whitman. Miller became their modern spokesman.

Transcendentalism not only provided Miller with a vital philosophy; it shaped his literary aesthetics and practice. He wrote essays and criticism in the high, personal manner of Emerson. As an unyielding satirist of materialism and the machine, he followed Thoreau. Like Whitman, he was a Dionysian singer, a celebrator of the senses, a cosmic outsider. Miller even patterned his greatest single literary work after Whitman's poetry. Although its celebration of America was inverted, *Tropic of Cancer* resembled "Song of Myself" in imagery, visions, and structure.

We think of Miller and Whitman as a century and a world apart. In fact, they were contemporaries and resi-

dents of the same city for a few months. Miller was born
the day after Christmas, 1891, in Manhattan, where
Whitman lay dying, barely able to autograph the final
edition of *Leaves of Grass,* his life's work. Miller would
not begin his life's work for forty-three years, but he
would always be linked to Whitman through the native
tradition in transcendentalism. He felt the force of that
affinity. In Miller's mind, Whitman was the "first white
aboriginal" and "only American teacher."[6] He identifies
his own plight as an artist with Whitman's "fight against
the powers that be, taking place as it did in the middle
and latter part of the Nineteenth Century."[7] He also
notes dissimilarities. Whitman "never used the language
of negation," Miller admits, "nor mocked, sneered at,
reviled or insulted other human beings," as Miller would
in his writing.[8] Nevertheless, Miller correctly identifies
himself more closely with Whitman than with any other
American writer, allying himself with the transcendental
America of Whitman. "For me," he writes, "Walt Whitman is a hundred, a thousand, times more *America* than
America itself."[9] As George Orwell first observed, however, "there is something rather curious in being
Whitman in the nineteen-thirties," because there is "a
radical difference between acceptance now and acceptance then." In the nineteenth century, individual freedom, self-reliance, and democracy were not remote ideals, Orwell argued; but by the thirties everything had
changed. Whitman had "died too early to see the deteri-
oration of American life that came with the rise of large-
scale industry and the exploiting of cheap immigrant la-
bour"; therefore, to be Whitman in "an epoch of fear,
tyranny, and regimentation," as Miller was doing, meant
that one had to accept "concentration camps, rubber
truncheons, Hitler, Stalin, bombs."[10] As we have seen,
however, Miller did not accept the cruelty or the dehu-
manized institutions of the modern state. He opposed
the spirit of the age, that drift of history into nightmare

that Orwell described. Miller's literary anarchy—he is
the best writer in this long, if unrecognized, tradition
since Thoreau—is exceedingly violent. By blasting
through the barbed wire of modern political oppression
at the personal level, Miller's literary anarchy reestab-
lishes Whitman's vision of an Adamic individual hero.

As befits the period, Miller's song of the self is
darker than Whitman's. The individual's experience in
America has changed and the self is virtually powerless
now; but by embracing his alienated status and placing
himself in opposition to his culture, Miller reinstates the
individual symbolically at the center of his society. Miller's song is more violent and pessimistic precisely because it is set in a world more hideous and inhuman than
the one Walt Whitman imagined. *Tropic of Cancer* recasts, rather than repeats, Whitman's "Song of Myself,"
but the underlying pattern of sensuous rebirth remains
intact.

Whitman begins "Song of Myself" with a self-
portrait. He is a middle-aged hero "in perfect health,"
content to "loafe." He holds all "creeds and schools in
abeyance." His single goal is to become one with nature
"without check with original energy."[11] Miller begins
Tropic of Cancer with a remarkably similar self-portrait.
He, too, is a middle-aged hero in "really superb health,"
loafing in Paris, rejecting all conventions, content to flow
with events.[12] For such heroes, there is never more
perfection than there is in the present moment. The
"procreant urge" is immediate and all-encompassing
("SM," 3). Miller lives wholly in the present, too, but his
procreant urge is more explicitly sexual.

As Whitman and Miller begin their songs, they
stand somewhat apart from their contemporary worlds.
Whitman declares that the latest "discoveries, inven-
tions, societies, authors old and new," as well as the
"horrors of fratricidal war," are not "the Me myself"
("SM," 4). Miller's isolation is more extreme. He is an

outsider who cannot welcome in all the elements of the age and declare with Whitman that "All goes onward and outward, nothing collapses" ("SM," 6). The entire world is in collapse for Miller; his "good solid animal health" is not reflected in the outer world, as it was so often for Walt Whitman (p. 45).

Whitman celebrates the urban experience, the "blab of the pave" and the "excited crowds," but Miller is ambivalent ("SM," 8). The modern metropolis is more an inferno than a paradiso. Both Miller and Whitman identify with the underside of respectable society, however, with what is "commonest, cheapest, nearest, easiest" ("SM," 14). Both are lusty and sensual—"hankering, gross, mystical, nude," says Whitman—and both laugh outright "at what you call dissolution" ("SM," 20). Miller and Whitman are poets of a bodily soul, of a sensual spirit. They "believe in the flesh and appetites"; they allow "forbidden voices / Voices of sexes and lusts" to speak through them; and they are both "fleshly, sensual, eating, drinking and breeding" creatures who are divine "inside and out" ("SM," 24). In this mystical inversion of values, the "scent of armpits" is "finer than prayer"; the individual is more important than "churches, bibles, and all creeds"; and the free, joyous being feels the "upward libidinous prongs" erupt in "seas of bright juice" which suffuse the earth ("SM," 24). The sexual act is rejuvenating and it is divine; it expresses and confirms individual power. The language of Whitman is only slightly less graphic than that of Miller.

An essential difference between these two transcendentalists is the darkness of Miller's world view. His leaves of grass are rotting. Miller must begin not by building a mythic America, but by tearing down the real America. Still, the new world he sees in the ruins is the same world of light Whitman saw. Whitman, too, underwent a dark night of the soul (far more truncated than Miller's) and emerged reborn as a "friendly and flowing savage" who implanted the seeds of "bigger and nimbler babes" and new nations, healed the sick and impotent, and created on equal footing with Jehovah, Zeus, Isis, and Buddha ("SM," 39–41). In Miller this superhuman rebirth leads to similar ends. After the "long dull misery" of ordinary life, Miller comes "face to face with the absolute" (p. 88). Finding God "insufficient," he is reborn as a savage "at the extreme limits of his spiritual being" (pp. 90, 147); and recognizing "no compulsion other than to create," Miller, the "gory sun god," begins to restore the dead to life (pp. 148, 228).

As these superhuman eruptions subside, there follows a quiet, steady reintegration of the self with the natural cycle. "I effuse my flesh in eddies, and drift in lacy jags," Whitman concludes. "I bequeath myself to the dirt to grow from the grass I love" ("SM," 52). Miller's conclusion mirrors Whitman's gentle lyricism: "I love everything that flows, everything that has time in it and becoming, that brings us back to the beginning where there is never end" (p. 233).

If Miller rejects America literally and figuratively, he still keeps the native, aboriginal self at the center of experience. The underlying pattern of individual growth and power has not changed since Whitman. In *Tropic of Cancer* the content and technique are modern, but the self-created image is not. Miller recasts himself in the mold of Whitman's great archetype, and in the process he creates new species of autobiography for his age.

It is finally as an autobiograpical artist that Miller was able to fuse his disparate literary achievements, and it is as an autobiographer that he takes his place in a major American tradition. The classic American autobiographies begin with the eighteenth-century masterpieces— Jonathan Edwards's *Personal Narrative* and Benjamin Franklin's *Autobiography*—proceed through Thoreau's *Walden* and Whitman's *Leaves of Grass*, and find twen-

tieth-century expression in the works of Henry Adams
and Henry Miller. Throughout this tradition there is a
concern with self-definition and self-creation, and there
is an increasing integration of the confessional genre
with contemporary forms of fiction and poetry. Miller's
autobiographical works take the genre of personal narration deep into the structure and strategies of modern fiction while retaining the essential elements of classic
American autobiography—a loose organic form, an exposition of ideas, the location of an autonomous self at
the center of our culture, and the cultivation of a contemporary voice of authority for the archetype of the free
individual in America.

Miller is America's most exhaustive classic autobiographer, although Walt Whitman is nearly his equal.
From midlife to a very old age, Whitman reworked the
story of his life, continually recreating the legend of himself in his poetry. Miller obeyed the autobiographical
impulse over roughly the same long period in his life,
but instead of creating a monumental palimpsest, as
Whitman did in *Leaves of Grass*, Miller generated a
fragmentary, ultimately circular series of distinct self-
creations. As Miller explains it, the form of his canon is
no more orderly than life itself, and at a deeper level
perfectly reflective of it:

In reading my books, which are purely autobiographical, one
should bear in mind that I write with one foot in the past. In
telling the story of my life I have frequently discarded the
chronological sequence in favor of the circular or spiral form of
progression. The time sequence which relates one event to another in linear fashion strikes me as falsely imitative of the true
rhythms of life. The facts and events which form the chain
of one's life are but starting points along the path of self-
discovery. I have endeavored to plot the inner pattern, follow
the potential being who was constantly deflected from his
course.[13]

Miller began what he would call his "interminable
autobiographical sleigh ride" in Paris.[14] "At a certain

point in my life I decided that henceforth I would write
about myself, my friends, my experiences, what I know
and what I had seen with my own eyes," Miller announced at the time. "Anything else, in my opinion, is
literature, and *I am not interested in literature*."[15] Of
course, autobiography of the sort Miller wrote *was* literature and, as he shaped it, appeared to be a radically
new form. The critics had some difficulty in classifying
Tropic of Cancer and subsequent works. Philip Rahv
wrote that Miller's "novels do in fact dissolve the forms
and genres of writing in a stream of exhortation, narrative, world-historical criticism, prose-poetry and spontaneous philosophy, all equally subjected to the strain and
grind of self-expression at all costs."[16] As recent literary
criticism focused on autobiography as a major genre of
imaginative writing, however, Miller's work became
more firmly categorized. David Littlejohn stated it simply: "Everything he has ever written is a piece of ever-
in-progress autobiography, a continuing *romanfleure* of
The Life of Henry Miller."[17] Miller himself had often
given the clue to critics about the genre of his works, although he misleadingly termed his autobiographies
"auto-novels" or "autobiographical novels":

The autobiographical novel, which Emerson predicted would
grow in importance with time, has replaced the great confessions. It is not a mixture of truth and fiction, this genre of literature, but an expansion and deepening of truth . . . truth di-
gested and assimilated. The being revealing himself does so on
all levels simultaneously.[18]

William Gordon, the first critic to investigate Miller
as a Romantic autobiographer, saw that the confessional
form allowed Miller to create "art out of the dramatiza-
tion of his own personality."[19] Subsequently, Gordon
also saw why Miller employed surrealism and other literary techniques of the avant-garde in autobiography:

In romantic autobiography especially, with its reconciling ten-
dencies, fantasy plays an important role. A man's needs, de-

sires, and wishes, and the fantasies which express them, as
well as reveries and dreams, which alter, however subtly, the
memory, all have the status of truth.[20]

Such a view brought into question the literal truth of
Miller's autobiographical confessions. Jay Martin, who
managed to write the definitive biography of Miller, a
formidable task indeed, comments that "all of Miller's
work constitutes the autobiography of his legend, not of
his life. His art is metamorphic, a creation of self based
on an obliteration or at least a masking of self."[21] This
discrepancy, however, between the literal author and
the literary hero, occurs in every autobiography. In a
self-creative genre, the author is creating a self that is
drawn from, but inevitably transcendent of, reality.
What makes Miller unusual among autobiographical artists is not his refusal to distinguish between art and life
(or between himself and his hero), but rather his use of
autobiography to transcend the art of autobiography itself. It is at this point that we address the most fundamental and perhaps enigmatic question which Miller's
achievement raises: what is the purpose of his autobiographical art?

William Gordon suggests that Miller's personal narration "could be embraced as the way simultaneously to
enhance life and to create it. The re-creation of life in the
past would become the means of living more fully in the
present."[22] Ihab Hassan carries this inquiry to its formal
limits and a bit beyond:

Miller turns literature into autobiography of a special kind; for
his work is less an effort to record and comprehend his life than
it is an attempt to *live* it, live it over and over again. . . . Unable
to redeem his life in art, he calls for a transcendence of both.
. . . In this sense, Henry Miller may be considered the first
author of anti-literature.[23]

Hassan argues that Miller aims to produce a pure form
out of the literal chaos of his life, a form that is itself
formless, an anti-art that is silent and points back to life
as the supreme art. This anti-art makes possible a unity

of "mind and nature, knowledge and experience, artist and man" that is impossible in any other genre of literature. In the transcendental vision, which Miller revives for a negative age, the "absolute negation" of art "becomes merely a pretext for total affirmation."[24]

Certainly Miller's art became more "artless" as his vision of himself deepened. Autobiography was the form in which he could not only most freely express "the struggle of the human being to emancipate himself, that is, to liberate himself from the prison of his own making," but also continually create himself anew until the very form and vehicle of that self-creation was superseded.[25] The monumental autobiography recording and administering this process of self-liberation gradually shed its skin as the author became more and more himself, less and less the artist. What remains before the reader is an extensive account of a single life spread over the twentieth century, vivid and lively, powerful and original. The autobiographies of Henry Miller illuminate the central issues of the age in a far more personal manner than any other author's work. The narratives, the essays, the criticism, the letters are what Henry Miller would have called *human* documents—eccentric, sprawling, explosive expressions of a life passing into art. Ultimately, these unparalleled life-writings do achieve what Henry Miller intended:

To be more direct and explicit, let me begin by stating what I sincerely believe my purpose to be in expressing myself through words. It is this: to reveal myself as openly, nakedly and unashamedly as possible. If I be asked why I would want to do this I can only answer—because my nature or my temperament compels me to do so. I am interested in life, all life, and every aspect of it. The one life I know best of all is my own. Examining my own life, describing it in detail, exposing it ruthlessly, I believe that I am rendering back life, enhanced and exalted, to those who read me. This seems to me a worthy task for a writer and one for which I have had illustrious predecessors.[26]

Notes

1. NEW YORK: EARLY SORROWS

1. See *Lawrence Durrell—Henry Miller: A Private Correspondence*, ed. George Wickes (New York: Dutton, 1963), p. 4; Jay Martin, *Always Merry and Bright: The Life of Henry Miller* (Santa Barbara, Calif.: Capra, 1978), pp. 304, 317; Edwin Muir, *The Present Age from 1914* (London, Cresset, 1939), p. 149; George Orwell, "Inside the Whale" (1940), rpt. in *Henry Miller: Three Decades of Criticism*, ed. Edward B. Mitchell (New York: New York University Press, 1971), pp. 24–25.

2. Henry Miller, Letter, *New Republic* (May 18, 1938); rpt. in *Henry Miller and the Critics*, ed. George Wickes (Carbondale: Southern Illinois University Press, 1963), p. 29.

3. Norman Mailer, *Genius and Lust: A Journey through the Major Writings of Henry Miller* (New York: Grove, 1976), pp. xiv, 4.

4. William A. Gordon, *Writer and Critic: A Correspondence with Henry Miller* (Baton Rouge: Louisiana State University, 1968), p. xv.

5. Ihab Habib Hassan, *The Literature of Silence: Henry Miller and Samuel Beckett* (New York: Knopf, 1967), pp. 30, 202.

6. Martin, p. 446.

7. Ibid., p. 20.

8. Henry Miller, letter to Emil Schnellock, March 20, 1922.

9. The manuscript of Miller's autobiographical account of his trip to Florida, written in 1928, was misplaced and

lost for many years, but now has been printed in Henry Miller, *Gliding into the Everglades and Other Essays* (Lake Oswego, Oregon: Lost Pleiade Press, 1977).

10. Gordon, p. xxix.

2. PARIS: BIRTH OF A WRITER

1. George Wickes, *Americans in Paris* (Garden City, New York: Doubleday, 1969), pp. 235–276.

2. Henry Miller, *Tropic of Cancer* (Paris: Obelisk, 1934; New York: Grove, 1961), p. 1. All further references to this work appear in the text.

3. Alfred Perlès, *My Friend Henry Miller: An Intimate Biography* (London: Spearman, 1955; New York: JohnDay, 1956), p. 14.

4. Jay Martin, *Always Merry and Bright: The Life of Henry Miller* (Santa Barbara, Calif.: Capra, 1978), p. 215.

5. Miller's "Mademoiselle Claude" was included in Peter Neagoe's *Americans Abroad* (1931), an anthology of works by Hemingway, Dos Passos, Pound, Aiken, Stein, and other expatriate writers.

6. Martin, p. 218.

7. Gunther Stuhlmann, ed., *Henry Miller: Letters to Anaïs Nin* (New York: Putnam's, 1965), p. 3.

8. Jack Kahane, *Memoirs of a Booklegger* (London: Joseph, 1939), as quoted in Stuhlmann, p. xviii.

9. Stuhlmann, pp. xiv–xv.

10. Burton Pike, "Time in Autobiography," *Comparative Literature*, 28, No. 4 (1976), 337.

11. Henry David Thoreau, *Walden and Civil Disobedience*, ed. Owen Thomas (New York: Norton Critical Edition, 1966), p. 61.

12. Kingsley Widmer, *Henry Miller* (New York: Twayne, 1963), p. 161.

13. Michael Fraenkel, "The Genesis of The Tropic of Cancer," in Bern Porter, ed., *The Happy Rock: A Book about Henry Miller* (Berkeley, Calif.: Porter, 1945), p. 47.

14. Edmund Wilson, "Twilight of the Expatriates," *New Republic*, XCIV (9 March 1938), 140; rpt. in *Henry Miller*

and the Critics, ed. George Wickes (Carbondale: Southern Illinois University, 1963), p. 26.

15.   Samuel Putnam, *Paris Was Our Mistress: Memoirs of a Lost and Found Generation* (New York: Viking, 1947); rpt. in *Henry Miller and the Critics,* pp. 11–15.

16.   Czeslaw Milosz, *Visions from San Francisco Bay,* trans. Richard Lourie (New York: Farrar Straus Giroux, 1982), pp. 138–140.

17.   See Kate Millett, *Sexual Politics* (Garden City, New York: Doubleday, 1970), and Frank Kermode, "Henry Miller and John Betjeman" (1963) in Edward B. Mitchell, ed., *Henry Miller: Three Decades of Criticism* (New York: New York University, 1971), pp. 85–95.

18.   See Harry Levin's remarks from "Commonwealth of Massachusetts vs. *Tropic of Cancer*" in *Henry Miller and the Critics,* pp. 168–174.

19.   Norman Mailer, *Genius and Lust: A Journey through the Major Writings of Henry Miller* (New York: Grove, 1976), p. 8.

20.   Letter of April, 1932, in Stuhlmann, pp. 40–42.

3.   Paris: Surrealism on the Seine

1.   Jay Martin, *Always Merry and Bright: The Life of Henry Miller* (Santa Barbara, Calif.: Capra, 1978), p. 311.

2.   Henry Miller, *What Are You Going to Do about Alf?* (Paris: Lecram-Servant, 1935; Berkeley, Calif.: Bern Porter, 1944—facsimile of 3rd Paris edition), p. 14.

3.   Martin, pp. 311–312.

4.   Ibid., p. 312.

5.   Ibid., p. 293.

6.   Gunther Stuhlmann, ed., *Henry Miller: Letters to Anaïs Nin* (New York: Putnam's, 1965), pp. 92, 119. The letters quoted are dated May and September, 1933.

7.   See Martin, pp. 294–296.

8.   Henry Miller, *Black Spring* (Paris: Obelisk, 1936; New York: Grove, 1963), p. 3. All further references to this work appear in the text.

9. George Wickes, *Americans in Paris* (Garden City, New York: Doubleday, 1969), pp. 270–271.

10. Martin, p. 293.

11. Kingsley Widmer, *Henry Miller* (New York: Twayne, 1963), pp. 41–46, 51.

12. Letter of November 28, 1933, in *Henry Miller: Letters to Anaïs Nin*, p. 127.

13. *Money and How It Gets That Way* was first printed in America by Bern Porter (Berkeley, Calif., 1945); rpt. in Henry Miller, *Stand Still Like the Hummingbird* (New York: New Directions, 1962), pp. 119–156.

14. Quoted by Miller in a letter to Nin; see Stuhlmann, p. 136.

15. Wickes, p. 271.

16. Miller, *Stand Still Like the Hummingbird*, p. 122.

17. Miller, "An Open Letter to Surrealists Everywhere" (1938); rpt. in Miller, *The Cosmological Eye* (Norfolk, Conn.: New Directions, 1939), pp. 156, 159, 160, 173–174.

18. *Scenario* and the other chapters of *Max and the White Phagocytes* are reprinted in *The Cosmological Eye*.

19. Miller, *The Cosmological Eye*, pp. 10–11.

20. Ibid., p. 356.

21. George Wickes, *Henry Miller*, University of Minnesota Pamphlets on American Writers, No. 56 (Minneapolis: University of Minnesota, 1966), p. 43.

22. Miller, *The Cosmological Eye*, p. 371.

4. PARIS: END OF AN ERA

1. Gunther Stuhlmann, ed., *Henry Miller: Letters to Anaïs Nin* (New York: Putnam's, 1965), p. 147.

2. Henry Miller, *Tropic of Capricorn* (Paris: Obelisk, 1939; New York: Grove, 1961), p. 10. All further references to this work appear in the text.

3. James M. Cox, *Mark Twain: The Fate of Humor* (Princeton: Princeton University, 1966), p. 169. The vernacular hero has been studied by Henry Nash Smith in *Mark Twain: The Development of a Writer* (Cambridge: Harvard University, 1962); the colloquial tradition

has been traced by Richard Bridgman in *The Colloquial Style in America* (New York: Oxford University, 1966). Clearly, Miller has made himself a modern vernacular hero; his native humor and voice make him a major figure in the American colloquial tradition.

4. Ibid., pp. 173, 177.

5. See Jay Martin, *Always Merry and Bright: The Life of Henry Miller* (Santa Barbara, Calif.: Capra, 1978), pp. 322–326, for a fuller account of these Dantesque affinities.

6. Miller names himself Gottlieb Leberecht Müller after the reborn amnesiac hero of a film by Werner Kraus, *A Man without a Name,* which Miller saw in Paris in 1932. See Martin, p. 323.

7. Love was a major theme in Miller's mind as he composed *Capricorn.* In the 1936 preface to this book, Miller had originally included these lines: "Even to unfold this story will be of no avail: at the best I shall earn the right to enter that Purgatory which we have made of life because we have ceased to love or even to understand the meaning of love." Sexual intercourse without love, while not condemned in *Tropic of Capricorn,* is nevertheless not an end in itself. Love is required if a paradise of the senses is to be reached. See Martin, p. 323.

8. William A. Gordon, *The Mind and Art of Henry Miller* (Kingsport, Tenn.: Louisiana State University, 1967), p. 111.

9. Henry Miller, *The World of Sex* (Paris: Olympia, 1959; New York: Grove, 1965), pp. 18–19. Written in March 1940, this personal review of his work and of the role of sex and obscenity in literature was privately printed and circulated by JHN (John Henry Nash) the same year. The Paris and later New York versions were considerably rewritten by Miller almost twenty years after.

5. GREECE: VOYAGE INTO LIGHT

1. Gunther Stuhlmann, ed., *Henry Miller: Letters to Anaïs Nin* (New York: Putnam's, 1965), p. 159.

2. Ibid., p. 160.

3. George Wickes, ed., *Lawrence Durrell—Henry Miller: A Private Correspondence* (New York: Dutton, 1963), p. 5. Letter is dated August, 1935.

4. Ibid., p. 153.

5. Ibid., pp. 157–158.

6. Henry Miller, *Tropic of Capricorn* (Paris: Obelisk, 1939; New York: Grove, 1961), p. 13.

7. "All these great birds of Tibet remind me of the Zen masters, who are up my street. Zen is my idea of life absolutely, the closest thing to what I am unable to formulate in words. I am a Zen addict through and through." Miller, letter to Durrell, March–April, 1939. See Wickes, p. 151. Miller accepted Zen philosophy except for "the monastic regime." At the same time, he despised most modern Zen or Buddhist leaders in Europe and America—"caricatures of the doctrine"—whom he found without evil, humor, magic, poetry, and life.

8. Stuhlmann, p. 157. This letter to Anaïs Nin was written February 21, 1939, three months before Miller left Paris and five months before he reached Greece.

9. Ihab Hassan, *The Literature of Silence: Henry Miller and Samuel Beckett* (New York: Knopf, 1967), pp. 83–84.

10. Henry Miller, *The Colossus of Maroussi* (San Francisco: Colt Press, 1941; New York: New Directions, 1941), pp. 4–5. All further references to the work appear in the text.

11. Stuhlmann, p. 187.

12. Ibid., p. 193.

13. Ibid., p. 193.

14. Henry Miller, "Reflections on Writing" (1940); rpt. in Lawrence Durrell, ed., *The Henry Miller Reader* (New York: New Directions, 1959), pp. 246–247.

15. Ibid., pp. 242–243.

6.   AMERICA: THE WAY HOME

1. Henry Miller, "Reunion in Brooklyn," *Sunday After the War* (Norfolk, Conn.: New Directions, 1944); rpt. in *The Henry Miller Reader,* ed. Lawrence Durrell (New York:

New Directions, 1959), pp. 95–96. All further references to this work appear in the text.

2. Miller, preface to "Reunion in Brooklyn," *The Henry Miller Reader*, p. 95.

3. Kinsley Widmer, *Henry Miller* (New York: Twayne, 1963), p. 98.

4. See Jay Martin, *Always Merry and Bright: The Life of Henry Miller* (Santa Barbara, Calif.: Capra, 1978), p. 534. This work, *Opus Pistorum* (New York: Grove, 1983), is sheer, if lighthearted, pornography featuring an amorous Casanova in Paris called John Thursday.

5. Miller, *Quiet Days in Clichy* (Paris: Olympia Press, 1956; New York: Grove, 1965). Both parts, "Quiet Days in Clichy" and "Mara-Marignan," were rewritten by Miller in 1956.

6. Miller, *The World of Sex* (New York: John Henry Nash, 1940; Chicago: Ben Abramson, 1941). A rewritten version was later published in France (Paris: Olympia, 1959) and in America (New York: Grove, 1965).

7. Gunther Stuhlmann, ed., *Henry Miller: Letters to Anaïs Nin* (New York: Putnam's, 1965), p. 200. This letter was written February 6, 1940, almost a year before Miller began his tour of America.

8. Ibid., p. 204.

9. Ibid., p. 228.

10. Ibid., p. 253.

11. Ibid., p. 262.

12. George Wickes, ed., *Lawrence Durrell—Henry Miller: A Private Correspondence* (New York: Dutton, 1963), p. 172.

13. Ibid., p. 173.

14. Ibid., p. 183.

15. Ibid., pp. 182–183.

16. Stuhlmann, p. 326.

17. Martin, p. 418.

18. Letter to Anaïs Nin, November 5, 1942, in Stuhlmann, p. 309.

19. Miller, *The Time of the Assassins: A Study of Rimbaud* (Norfolk, Conn.: New Directions, 1956). Originally published as two essays in *New Directions* annuals No. 9, No.

11 (1946, 1949). All further references to this work appear in the text.

20. Stuhlmann, p. 337.
21. Ibid., pp. 337–338.

7.   BROOKLYN: THE ONE GREAT STORY

1.   Ihab Hassan, *The Literature of Silence: Henry Miller and Samuel Beckett* (New York: Knopf, 1967), p. 85.
2.   Henry Miller, *Sexus,* Book 1 of *The Rosy Crucifixion* (Paris: Obelisk Press, 1949; New York: Grove, 1965), p. 9. All further references to this work appear in the text.
3.   Henry Miller, *Plexus,* Book 2 of *The Rosy Crucifixion* (Paris: Olympia, 1953; New York: Grove, 1965), p. 52. All further references to this work appear in the text.
4.   George Wickes, ed., *Lawrence Durrell—Henry Miller: A Private Correspondence* (New York: Dutton, 1963), p. 334.
5.   Henry Miller, *Nexus,* Book 3 of *The Rosy Crucifixion* (Paris: Obelisk Press, 1960; New York: Grove, 1965), p. 165. All further references to this work appear in the text.
6.   George Wickes, ed., pp. 262–263.
7.   Ibid., pp. 264–265.
8.   Ibid., p. 267.
9.   Ibid., pp. 268–269.

8.   BIG SUR: PARADISE AND BEYOND

1.   Jay Martin, *Always Merry and Bright: The Life of Henry Miller* (Santa Barbara, Calif.: Capra, 1978), p. 434.
2.   Henry Miller, *The Books in My Life* (Norfolk, Conn.: New Directions, 1952), p. 11. All further references to this work appear in the text.
3.   Henry Miller, *Big Sur and the Oranges of Hieronymus Bosch* (New York: New Directions, 1957), p. 3. All further references to this work appear in the text.
4.   See Mildred Edie Brady, "The New Cult of Sex and Anarchy," *Harper's Magazine,* 194 (April, 1947), 312–322.

Apparently this and similar articles prompted a number of pilgrimages to Miller's austere cabin on Partington Ridge, although Ms. Brady's account of life among the artists of Big Sur is not sensationalized and is an interesting argument that the region could become "a new Paris" for writers.

5. First published as a separate volume: Henry Miller, *A Devil in Paradise* (New York: Signet/New American Library, 1956).

6. Martin, p. 430.

7. Sir Herbert Read, rev. of *Big Sur and the Oranges of Hieronymus Bosch*, by Henry Miller, *The New Statesman*, 40 (March 29, 1958), 410.

8. Phoebe Adams, rev. of *Big Sur and the Oranges of Hieronymus Bosch*, by Henry Miller, *Atlantic Magazine*, 200 (August 1957), p. 82.

9. Alfred Perlès, *My Friend Henry Miller: An Intimate Biography* (London: Spearman, 1955).

10. Henry Miller, *Mother, China, and the World Beyond* (Santa Barbara, Calif.: Capra, 1977). This was the forty-first and final volume in the Capra Chapbook Series; the first volume was also by Miller (*On Turning Eighty*, 1972).

11. Ibid., p. 26.

12. See Jay Martin, p. 459.

13. George Wickes, ed., *Lawrence Durrell—Henry Miller: A Private Correspondence* (New York: Dutton, 1963).

14. Henry Miller's letters to Barney Rosset are quoted in Martin, pp. 462–463.

15. Martin, p. 473.

16. The exhaustive account of this case is E. R. Hutchison, Tropic of Cancer *on Trial: A Case History of Censorship* (New York: Grove, 1968). See also Charles Rembar, *The End of Obscenity: The Trials of* Lady Chatterley, Tropic of Cancer, *and* Fanny Hill (New York: Random House, 1968), pp. 168–215, and Elmer Gertz, *A Handful of Clients* (Chicago: Follett, 1965), pp. 229–303. Rembar was chief lawyer and president of Grove Press; Gertz defended Miller's books before the Illinois Supreme Court.

17. Martin, p. 475.

18. Henry Miller, *My Life and Times* (Chicago: Playboy Press, 1971).

19. The best interview is that by George Wickes, "Henry Miller," in *Writers at Work: The Paris Review Interviews*, Second Series (New York: Viking, 1963), pp. 165–191. See also Georges Belmont, *Henry Miller in Conversation with Georges Belmont*, trans. Antony Macnabb and Harry Scott (New York: Quadrangle, 1972); Robert Snyder, *This Is Henry, Henry Miller from Brooklyn: Conversations with the Author from* The Henry Miller Odyssey [a film by Snyder] (Los Angeles: Nash, 1974); and Bernard Wolfe, "Playboy Interviews: Henry Miller," *Playboy Magazine*, 11 (September 1964), pp. 77–94.

20. In addition to the two indispensable books of Miller's letters to Durrell and to Nin, frequently cited elsewhere in this book, see the following fine collections of correspondence: Henry Miller, *Semblance of a Devoted Past* (Berkeley, Calif.: Porter, 1944)—letters to Emil Schnellock; William A. Gordon, *Writer and Critic: A Correspondence with Henry Miller* (Baton Rouge: Louisiana State University, 1968); Elmer Gertz and Felice F. Lewis, ed., *Henry Miller: Years of Trial and Triumph, 1962–1964, The Correspondence of Henry Miller and Elmer Gertz* (Carbondale: Southern Illinois University, 1978); and Lawrence Durrell, Alfred Perlès, and Henry Miller, *Art and Outrage: A Correspondence about Henry Miller* (London: Putnam, 1959; New York: Dutton, 1961).

21. Henry Miller, *Insomnia: Or, the Devil at Large* (Garden City, New York: Doubleday, 1974).

22. Henry Miller, *On Turning Eighty* (Santa Barbara, Calif.: Capra, 1972).

23. Henry Miller, *Henry Miller's Book of Friends: A Tribute to Friends of Long Ago* (Santa Barbara, Calif.: Capra, 1976).

24. Henry Miller, *My Bike and Other Friends* (Santa Barbara, Calif.: Capra, 1978).

25. Henry Miller, *Joey: A Loving Portrait of Alfred Perlès*

Together with Some Bizarre Episodes Relating to the Opposite Sex (Santa Barbara, Calif.: Capra, 1979).

26. Ibid., pp. 53–54.
27. Ibid., p. 126.
28. Henry Miller, *The World of Lawrence: A Passionate Appreciation*, ed. Evelyn J. Hinz and John J. Teunissen (Santa Barbara, Calif.: Capra, 1980). Perhaps the most lavish posthumous commemorative volume to date is Henry Miller, *The Paintings of Henry Miller: Paint as You Like and Die Happy* (San Francisco: Chronicle Books, 1982), which includes essays by Miller, Durrell, and Noel Young, as well as reproductions of watercolors and drawings from 1930–1980.
29. Ibid., pp. 138–139.
30. Ibid., p. 27.
31. Ibid., p. 139.
32. James Laughlin, "A Tribute," in *Dictionary of Literary Biography Yearbook: 1980*, ed. Karen L. Rood, Jean W. Ross, and Richard Ziegfeld (Detroit: Gale, 1981), p. 78.

9. AUTOBIOGRAPHY IN AMERICA

1. Henry Miller, "Reflections on Writing" (1940); rpt. in Lawrence Durrell, ed., *The Henry Miller Reader* (New York: New Directions, 1959), p. 250.
2. George Orwell, "Inside the Whale" (1940); rpt. in George Wickes, ed., *Henry Miller and the Critics* (Carbondale: Southern Illinois University, 1963), p. 37.
3. The colloquial tradition in American literature is traced by Richard Bridgman in *The Colloquial Style in America* (New York: Oxford University, 1966). The vernacular tradition is discussed by Henry Nash Smith in *Mark Twain: The Development of a Writer* (Cambridge, Mass.: Harvard University, 1962).
4. Ihab Hassan, *The Literature of Silence: Henry Miller and Samuel Beckett* (New York: Knopf, 1967), p. 45.
5. Among the few studies that focus on Miller's affinity to the nineteenth-century transcendentalists are: Edward J.

Rose, "The Aesthetics of Civil Disobedience: Henry Miller, Twentieth-Century Transcendentalist," *Edge,* 1, No. 1 (1963), 5–16; and Arnold Smithline, "Henry Miller and the Transcendental Spirit," *Emerson Society Quarterly,* 43, No. 1 (1966), 50–56.

6. Henry Miller, *The Books in My Life* (1952; rpt. New York: New Directions, 1969), pp. 233–234.

7. Ibid., p. 238.

8. Ibid., pp. 238–239.

9. Ibid., p. 104.

10. Orwell, "Inside the Whale," pp. 39–40.

11. Walt Whitman, "Song of Myself," *Leaves of Grass,* Norton Critical Edition, ed. by Sculley Bradley and Harold W. Blodgett (New York: New York University, 1965), section 1 of 1891–1892 edition; hereafter cited in the text as "SM" followed by the section number of the poem.

12. Henry Miller, *Tropic of Cancer* (1934; rpt. New York: Grove, 1961), p. 45. All further references to this work appear in the text.

13. Henry Miller, *The World of Sex* (1940; rev. ed. New York: Grove, 1965), pp. 83–84.

14. Henry Miller, "My Life as an Echo," in *Stand Still Like the Hummingbird* (New York: New Directions, 1962), p. 84.

15. Henry Miller, "An Open Letter to Surrealists Everywhere" (1938); rpt. in *The Cosmological Eye* (Norfolk, Conn.: New Directions, 1939), p. 161.

16. Philip Rahv, "Sketches in Criticism: Henry Miller" (1949); rpt. in Wickes, *Henry Miller and the Critics,* p. 82.

17. David Littlejohn, "The Tropics of Miller" (1962); rpt. in Edward Mitchell, ed., *Henry Miller: Three Decades of Criticism* (New York: New York University, 1971), p. 103.

18. Miller, *The Books in My Life,* p. 169.

19. William A. Gordon, *The Mind and Art of Henry Miller* (Kingsport, Tenn.: Louisiana State University, 1967), p. 52.

20. William A. Gordon, *Writer and Critic: A Correspon-*

dence with Henry Miller (Baton Rouge: Louisiana State University, 1968), p. xiii.

21. Jay Martin, *Always Merry and Bright: The Life of Henry Miller* (Santa Barbara, Calif.: Capra, 1978), p. vii.

22. Gordon, *The Mind and Art of Henry Miller,* p. 47.

23. Hassan, p. 30.

24. Ibid., pp. 66, 78.

25. Miller, *The Books in My Life,* p. 125.

26. Henry Miller, "Obscenity in Literature" (1957); rpt. in *Henry Miller on Writing* (New York: New Directions, 1964), pp. 193–194.

Bibliography

1.   WORKS BY HENRY MILLER

Tropic of Cancer. Paris: Obelisk, 1934; New York: Grove, 1961.

What Are You Going to Do about Alf? Paris: Lecram-Servant, 1935; Berkeley, Calif.: Porter, 1944; London: Turret, 1971.

Aller Retour New York. Paris: Obelisk, 1935.

Black Spring. Paris: Obelisk, 1936; New York: Grove, 1963.

Scenario (A Film with Sound). Paris: Obelisk, 1937.

Money and How It Gets That Way. Paris: Booster, 1938; Berkeley, Calif.: Porter, 1945.

Max and the White Phagocytes. Paris: Obelisk, 1938.

The Cosmological Eye. Norfolk, Conn.: New Directions, 1939.

Tropic of Capricorn. Paris: Obelisk, 1939; New York: Grove, 1961.

The World of Sex. Chicago: Abramson, 1940; New York: Grove, 1965.

The Colossus of Maroussi. San Francisco: Colt, 1941.

The Wisdom of the Heart. Norfolk, Conn.: New Directions, 1941.

Sunday After the War. Norfolk, Conn.: New Directions, 1944.

The Air-Conditioned Nightmare. New York: New Directions, 1945.

Maurizius Forever. Waco, Texas: Motive, 1946; San Francisco: Colt, 1946.

Remember to Remember. New York: New Directions, 1947.

The Smile at the Foot of the Ladder. New York: Duell, Sloan, and Pearce, 1948.

Sexus. Book 1 of *The Rosy Crucifixion*. Paris: Obelisk, 1949; New York: Grove, 1965.

The Books in My Life. London: Owen, 1952; Norfolk, Conn.: New Directions, 1952.

Plexus. Book 2 of *The Rosy Crucifixion*. (French version) Paris: Corrêa, 1952; (English version) Paris: Olympia, 1953; New York: Grove, 1965.

Nights of Love and Laughter. Ed. Kenneth Rexroth. New York: Signet/New American Library, 1955.

The Time of the Assassins: A Study of Rimbaud. Norfolk, Conn.: New Directions, 1956.

Quiet Days in Clichy. Paris: Olympia, 1956; New York: Grove, 1965.

A Devil in Paradise. New York: Signet/New American Library, 1956.

Big Sur and the Oranges of Hieronymus Bosch. New York: New Directions, 1957.

The Henry Miller Reader. Ed. Lawrence Durrell. New York: New Directions, 1959.

The Intimate Henry Miller. Ed. Lawrence Clark Powell. New York: Signet/New American Library, 1959.

Nexus. Book 3 of *The Rosy Crucifixion*. Paris: Obelisk, 1960; New York: Grove, 1965.

To Paint Is to Love Again. Alhambra, Calif.: Cambia, 1960.

Stand Still Like the Hummingbird. Norfolk, Conn.: New Directions, 1962.

Just Wild About Harry: A Melo Melo in Seven Scenes. New York: New Directions, 1963.

Henry Miller on Writing. Ed. Thomas H. Moore. New York: New Directions, 1964.

Insomnia; Or, the Devil at Large. Euclid, Ohio: Loujon, 1971.

My Life and Times. Chicago: Playboy, 1971.

On Turning Eighty; Journey to an Antique Land; Foreword to "The Angel Is My Watermark." Santa Barbara, Calif.: Capra, 1972.

Reflections on the Death of Mishima. Santa Barbara, Calif.: Capra, 1972.

First Impressions of Greece. Santa Barbara, Calif.: Capra, 1973.

Henry Miller's Book of Friends: A Tribute to Friends of Long Ago. Santa Barbara, Calif.: Capra, 1976.

Mother, China, and the World Beyond. Santa Barbara, Calif.: Capra, 1977.

Gliding into the Everglades. Lake Oswego, Oregon: Lost Pleiade Press, 1977.

My Bike and Other Friends. Volume 2 of *Book of Friends*. Santa Barbara, Calif.: Capra, 1978.

Joey: A Loving Portrait of Alfred Perlès Together with Some Bizarre Episodes Relating to the Opposite Sex. Volume 3 of *Book of Friends*. Santa Barbara, Calif.: Capra, 1979.

The World of Lawrence: A Passionate Appreciation. Ed. Evelyn J. Hinz and John J. Teunissen. Santa Barbara, Calif.: Capra, 1980.

The Paintings of Henry Miller: Paint As You Like and Die Happy. San Francisco: Chronicle Books, 1982.

2.   CORRESPONDENCE

Durrell, Lawrence, Alfred Perlès, and Henry Miller. *Art and Outrage: A Correspondence about Henry Miller*. London: Putnam, 1959; New York: Dutton, 1961.

Fowlie, Wallace, ed. *Letters of Henry Miller and Wallace Fowlie, 1943–1972*. New York: Grove, 1975.

Gertz, Elmer, and Felice F. Lewis. *Henry Miller: Years of Trial and Triumph, 1962–1964, The Correspondence of Henry Miller and Elmer Gertz*. Carbondale: Southern Illinois University, 1978.

Miller, Henry. *Order and Chaos chez Hans Reichel*. Tucson, Ariz.: Loujon, 1966.

———. *The Waters Reglitterized*. San Jose, Calif.: John Kiddis, 1950.

———, and Michael Fraenkel. *Hamlet*. Vol. 1, Santurce, Puerto Rico: Carrefour, 1939. Vol. 2, New York: Carrefour, 1941. Rev. ed., *The Michael Fraenkel-Henry Miller Correspondence Called Hamlet*. London: Edition du Laurier/Carrefour, 1962.

———, and William A. Gordon. *Writer and Critic: A Correspondence with Henry Miller*. Baton Rouge: Louisiana State University, 1968.

———, and Emil Schnellock. *Semblance of a Devoted Past*. Berkeley, Calif.: Porter, 1944.

————, and Brenda Venus. *Dear, Dear Brenda: The Love Letters of Henry Miller to Brenda Venus*. New York: Morrow, 1986.

Stuhlmann, Gunther, ed. *Letters to Anaïs Nin*. New York: Putnam's, 1965.

White, Emil, ed. *Henry Miller—Between Heaven and Hell, A Symposium*. Holland: N.V. Drukkerij G.T. Thieme, 1961; Big Sur, 1961.

Wickes, George, ed. *Lawrence Durrell—Henry Miller: A Private Correspondence*. New York: Dutton, 1963.

Wood, Richard Clement, ed. *Collector's Quest: The Correspondence of Henry Miller and J. Rives Childs, 1947–65*. Charlottesville: University Press of Virginia, 1968.

3. INTERVIEWS

Belmont, Georges. *Henry Miller in Conversation with Georges Belmont*. Trans. Antony Macnabb and Harry Scott. New York: Quadrangle, 1972.

Grauer, Ben. *Henry Miller Recalls and Reflects*. Phonodisc. Modern Voice Series. New York: Riverside Records, 1956.

Snyder, Robert, dir. *Henry Miller: Reflections on Writing*. Film. Los Angeles, 1971.

————. *This Is Henry, Henry Miller from Brooklyn: Conversations with the Author from* The Henry Miller Odyssey. Los Angeles: Nash, 1974.

Wickes, George. "Henry Miller." In *Writers at Work: The Paris Review Interviews*. 2nd series. New York: Viking, pp. 165–191.

Wolfe, Bernard. "Playboy Interview: Henry Miller." *Playboy Magazine*, 11, No. 9 (Sept. 1964), pp. 77–94.

4. BIBLIOGRAPHIES

Moore, Thomas H. *Bibliography of Henry Miller*. Minneapolis: Henry Miller Literary Society, 1961.

Porter, Bernard H. *Henry Miller: A Chronology and Bibliography*. Baltimore: Waverly, 1945.

Renken, Maxine. *Bibliography of Henry Miller, 1945–1961*. Swallow Pamphlets No. 12. Denver: Swallow, 1962.

Shifreen, Lawrence J. *Henry Miller: A Bibliography of Secondary Sources*. Metuchen, N.J.: Scarecrow, 1979.

5. BIOGRAPHIES

Baxter, Annette Kar. *Henry Miller, Expatriate*. Critical Essays in English and American Literature, 5. Pittsburgh: University of Pittsburgh, 1961.

Hutchison, E. R. Tropic of Cancer *on Trial: A Case History of Censorship*. New York: Grove, 1968.

Martin, Jay. *Always Merry and Bright: The Life of Henry Miller*. Santa Barbara, Calif.: Capra, 1978.

Perlès, Alfred. *My Friend Henry Miller: An Intimate Biography*. London: Spearman, 1955; New York: Day, 1956.

Powell, Lawrence Clark. "The Miller of Big Sur." *Books in My Baggage: Adventures in Reading and Collecting*. Cleveland: World Publishing, 1960, pp. 148–153.

Schmiele, Walter. *Henry Miller in Selbstzeugnissen und Bilddokumenten*. Hamburg: Rowohlt, 1961.

Vandenbergh, John. *Kleine Biografie van Henry Miller*. Rotterdam: Donker, 1961.

6. CRITICISM

Gordon, William A. *The Mind and Art of Henry Miller*. Kingsport, Tenn.: Louisiana State University, 1967.

Hassan, Ihab Habib. *The Literature of Silence: Henry Miller and Samuel Beckett*. New York: Knopf, 1967.

A Henry Miller Miscellanea. San Mateo, Calif.: Porter, 1945.

Mailer, Norman. *Genius and Lust: A Journey through the Major Writings of Henry Miller*. New York: Grove, 1976.

Mitchell, Edward B., ed. *Henry Miller: Three Decades of Criticism*. New York: New York University, 1971.

Nelson, Jane A. *Form and Image in the Fiction of Henry Miller*. Detroit: Wayne State University, 1970.

Of, By, and About Henry Miller: A Collection of Pieces by Miller and Others. Yonkers, New York: Alicat, 1947.

Porter, Bern, ed. *The Happy Rock: A Book About Henry Miller*. Berkeley, Calif.: Packard, 1945.

Wickes, George, ed. *Henry Miller and the Critics*. Carbondale: Southern Illinois University, 1963.

———. *Henry Miller*. University of Minnesota Pamphlets on American Writers, No. 56. Minneapolis: University of Minnesota, 1966.

———. *Americans in Paris*. Garden City, N.Y.: Doubleday, 1969, pp. 234–276.

Widmer, Kingsley. *Henry Miller*. Twayne's U.S. Authors Series, No. 44. New York: Twayne, 1963.

Index